Keep Smiling Through...

The Story of Hambleden

1939-1945

Chris Whitehead

The cover image is of Jim Tilbury and Reg Skates fishing in the brook outside the Bakery in about 1941 © Jim Tilbury

Birch Cottage Publications

Pheasants Hill

Hambleden

RG9 6 SN

chriswhiteheadhambleden@gmail.com

© 2025 This publication is in copyright. No reproduction of any part may take place without the written permission of the author.

ISBN 978-1-916838-32-1

Produced by Biddles Books Limited, Kings Lynn, Norfolk

A RECENT PHOTOGRAPH OF HAMBLEDEN. IT HAS BARELY CHANGED SINCE 1945.

At 11.15am on 3 September 1939, the Prime Minister, Neville Chamberlain, addressed the nation by radio:

> *This morning the British ambassador in Berlin handed the German government a final note stating that unless we heard from them by 11 o'clock, that they were prepared at once to withdraw their troops from Poland, a state of war would exist between us. I have to tell you now that no such undertaking has been received, and that consequently this country is at war with Germany.*

Contents

1.	Hambleden	6
2.	Keep Calm and Carry On	10
3.	Persons of Significance	24
4.	Food & Rationing	37
5.	Children, Evacuees & the School	46
6.	Home Guard	63
7.	Entertainment	68
8.	Fawley Court	78
9.	National Trust	87
10.	War & the Church	89
11.	Victory	101
12.	Afterwards	108

Appendices	1. Kelly's Directory	109
	2. Hambleden Village	110
	3. Surrender of Japan	111
	4. We'll Meet Again	113
	5. Roll of Honour	114

Chapter 1

Hambleden

Hambleden is a small rural community roughly equidistant between Marlow and Henley, about a mile north of the A4155 at Mill End. Its most prominent natural feature is a brook that runs through the village, under two bridges, and on to the Thames. Although the village is in Buckinghamshire, Henley on Thames, in Oxfordshire, has always been its main commercial centre. In 1931 it had a population of 1,257. Even by modern standards, Hambleden is rural. In 1939, when only a very few inhabitants owned a motor car, it was even more so.

I have attempted to look into the story of the village during the period of the Second World War (the War) using the verbatim recollections of two residents who were children at the time: Jim Tilbury (JT) and Evelyn Robinson (ER). Another resident who was a teenager at the time, Charles Gray (CG), has written about life in the village in his book *'Born on Chiltern Slopes'* (2003). I have borrowed some of his text. Rector Wilfred Watts' (WW) booklet *'A Village Parson'* (1979) has also provided an invaluable insight. I have been most fortunate to have had access to the Parish Magazines, the school's Admission Register, and the Headmaster's Journal for the period, sections of which are reproduced below, indicating the year and month of the record.

When writing these paragraphs, I have been conscious of the fact that, eighty years on, we know how the War ended – a luxury not afforded to those who lived in Hambleden between 1939 and 1945. They could neither tell how long it would go on for, nor who would win in the end. It was a troubling time.

Gray Joliffe designed the front and back covers. My wife, Jo, and my friend Peter Steward read the first drafts of the text and suggested valuable improvements. I thank them all.

****

The outbreak of war did not come as a surprise. Tensions in Europe had been building for years and there was a growing feeling that German aggression needed to be confronted with force. Most Britons were desperate to avoid the destruction of another world war, a view shared by Chamberlain. In an attempt at appeasement, he had met with Hitler in Munich in September 1938, and had returned, waving his controversial 'peace for our time' document.

The British population had expected an imminent war, and Chamberlain's peace pledge was at first greeted with acclaim, but this generally positive reaction quickly soured. Appeasement had its limits. Once Britain began to see that Germany had no intention of sticking to the Munich agreement, the tone of British policy began to change.

The country began to accept, with some reluctance, that war was necessary to stop Hitler. They were resigned to the fact that Germany had to be stopped by force. There was none of the flag waving patriotism of August 1914. Many people could remember the reasons for going to war in 1914 - to defend the balance of power in Europe and safeguard Britain's position in the world. Now, only twenty-five years later, those reasons were real again; but this time the threat was more tangible, was closer to home – the country had to defend itself from a likely German invasion.

As Churchill[1], rather stirringly, put it in June 1940...

> .... *the Battle of France is over. I expect that the Battle of Britain is about to begin. Upon this battle depends the survival of Christian civilization. Upon it depends our own British life, and the long continuity of our institutions and our Empire. The whole fury and might of the enemy must very soon be turned on us. Hitler knows that he will have to break us in this island or lose the war. If we can stand up to him, all Europe may be free and the life of the world may move forward into broad, sunlit uplands. But if we fail, then the whole world, including the United States, including all that we have known and cared for, will sink into the abyss of a new Dark Age made more sinister, and perhaps more protracted, by the lights of perverted science. Let us therefore brace ourselves to our duties, and so bear ourselves that, if the British Empire and its Commonwealth last for a thousand years, men will still say, "This was their finest hour."*

******

---

[1] He had become Prime Minister in May 1940.

The villagers of Hambleden received the news with their usual stoicism. They made up a community in which the Church and the Rector, Canon Wilfred Watts, were at the centre. The Rector described what it meant to live in a rural parish....

....For centuries the Parish Church has been symbolical of village life. Around it has revolved the activities, both religious and secular, which make up the communal life - so important and so integral a part of the English character. Of late, the call of the town and the improved means of communication between one centre and another have to some extent, loosened the ties of the Country Parish and have removed some of the characteristics of county life. Yet, the Country Parish still remains - in times of greatest stress and misery - the bulwark of genuine life and of true and lasting principles.

In a large town the individual is apt to become an impersonal cog in a machine-made wheel. He loses his personality in the colourless plan of town life. In the Country Parish he is still an integral part of the general scheme. What he thinks and what he does matters to everyone. His family life, his home and his garden can play an important part in the pattern which make up the village as a whole. His participation in parish policy can influence the welfare of those to whom he is related, or with whom he is in close friendship, to a great extent. Consequently, he is a live and important person.

All over the country there are others like him - others who understand how to live and how to appreciate the beauty and reality of country life ; of nature and of simple and genuine living.

1941.7

THE VILLAGE PUMP IN THE FORTIES

The picture the Rector paints may seem idyllic, for it was only during the 1950s that mains water and drains arrived in Hambleden. Prior to that, residents had relied on the village pump, set between two chestnut trees in the centre of the village. Many houses had their own wells; some collected rainwater. Animals generally drank from the brook.

JT remembers villagers from Ibstone coming to Hambleden with two horses pulling a bowser to take water back up the hill to their village.

Electricity became generally available in the village from the 1930s, though not everyone was wired up. The Rector remembered that the Verger (Mr Cook, or Verger Cook[2] as he was commonly called) had to light about a dozen oil lamps in the church, and twice that number in the winter.

ER remembers...

---

[2] Verger Cook would cut the grass in the churchyard with a scythe.

.....There were regular deliveries to the villages of paraffin for the paraffin (Aladdin) heaters. Oil too – the oil man (Giles) came around with his van and oil lamps with their long wicks[3]. Accumulators[4] were also delivered so you could keep your radio working. You would swap out your battery and pay him. Some were large batteries where you moved the plugs along each section when one went flat. Smaller ones were about 2 volts for the radio.

---

[3] He also sold all sorts of household goods – buckets, mops, pans etc.

[4] An accumulator is an energy storage device that accepts, stores, and releases energy as needed. Some accumulators accept energy over a long period of time and release it over a short period of time. Two-volt accumulators were used to power the valve heaters in wireless sets.

Chapter 2

Keep Calm and Carry On

The Parish Magazines reveal a life in which the Church and the villagers desperately tried to continue life as normal during the War, but, of course, they couldn't. Even in a rural hamlet like Hambleden the War impacted on peoples' lives – and not only because many of the men and women were called away to serve in the armed forces. Almost every copy of the Magazine has a paragraph or two about a local man who was missing or had been taken as a POW. One of those killed[5] in action was Jim Tilbury's uncle Frank, who died while serving in the desert, when he drove his motorbike into the side of a Bren gun carrier in the dark.

And, of course, several local young men were conscripted:

> *During 1941, an air training corps was formed in Henley, 447 Squadron. I, at the age of seventeen, became one of the first members of the squadron. We were issued with Air Force blue uniform which made me feel very special. We had a bugle and drum band which paraded round the town at every opportunity. My first flight was in a small aircraft at the top of White Hill in Remenham. I was called up in 1942 and was posted to India, but*

---

[5] A complete list of men from Hambleden who lost their lives in the War is included as an appendix. Full details of their lives can be found in a Book of Remembrance in the Church.

was not demobbed until one and a half years after the surrender of Japan.   CG

WW remembered that Hambleden suffered far more than elsewhere....

....The police reported that over a hundred large bombs fell within a mile of Hambleden village.[6] Perhaps the German pilots mistook us for the RAF camp at Medmenham. Many windows were broken. Four were smashed in the church, including the wonderful East window. Lord and Lady Hambleden lent the church a vast, beautiful, red velvet curtain to cover the window. The roof of the church had to be covered in places.

Jim Tilbury remembers...

...Royal Engineers worked at the end of Ferry Lane practicing putting Bailey Bridges up across the river. They had a camp round by Couch Field Barn, along the carriage drive. They used to camp there and throw flashes in the pond and catch the trout.

They would test the Bailey Bridge with a tank. Someone had family in Bisham, so he went home to Marlow in his tank, along the main road, down the High Street, across the Bridge and into Bisham!   JT

---

[6] Over a hundred? 'Bombs over Bucks' on the Bucks CC website shows only two bombs falling on Hambleden, another on Pheasants Hill and another on Colstrope. Perhaps the Rector meant the phosphorous flares that JT refers to in his memories.

The Women's Institute and the Mothers' Union continued to meet each month. The WI, then as now, specialised in jam making. In 1940 they were able to boast that, although it was ......

> ....*not possible to give the exact results of our jam-making, but 8 cwts. of sugar have been used and at least 1,600 lbs. of jam and jelly have been made of which 1,000 lbs. have already been sold*   1940.6

8 cwts. of sugar! Almost 900 lbs! Quite remarkable in wartime!

Other WI activities might include .....

> *.... a demonstration on re-footing stockings, and making mittens out of old socks.*   1941.4

The cricket club struggled to maintain its fixture list....

> *....The cricket season finished on September 2nd. We cannot say we had a good season. First the weather was not too kind to us, then the War called for five of our members and we wish them the best of luck. Nineteen matches were fixed, ten were lost, six won, and three scratched.*   1939.10

The football team seemed more fortunate.....

> *... Our football team is doing excellently. Six matches have been played and four won. Men home on leave are asked to let the committee know if they want a game. A place in the team will always be found for them.*   1940.12

Having lain dormant since the Great War, the Hambleden Cottage Garden Show was reinstated....

> ....The Hambleden Cottage Garden Show achieved distinction in two directions. It was probably the only show of its kind in the country to be held : it ended in the course of one War and was resuscitated in another. The 'business as usual' spirit of the committee in deciding to carry on was amply justified and spoke volumes for their confidence.   1939.10

The show flourished so that ....

> ....On August 29th, one of the few hot days of a disappointing month, the Flower and Vegetable Show was held in the Parish Room. The attendance was very encouraging and the show itself a remarkably good one. We cannot do better than quote the following paragraph which appeared in the Henley and South Oxfordshire Standard in order to make it clear to our readers that the annual function is taken seriously by experts in the horticultural world :

> ' Record entries and a big improvement in the quality of the exhibits and the manner in which they were staged marked the show held by the Hambleden Cottage Garden Society at the Parish Room, Hambleden, on Saturday last. The entries totalled 357 - over a hundred more than last year and 164 more than in 1940. It was in 1940 that the show was revived after a lapse of some thirty years, and the faith and enterprise of those

> *responsible for this are reaping a reward in the shape of improved crops, both from the point of view of quality and quantity. This is just what the organisers had in mind when the society was re-started, and the success they have achieved rather tends to prove, as one of the judges stated on Saturday, that these small and intimate shows help to foster interest in horticulture, and at the same time do a great deal to help the dig-for-victory campaign.'*   1942.9

The village had always donated potatoes to Henley Cottage Hospital[8], but the bad winter of 1940 meant that the WI would report that .....

> *....The potato growing effort resulted in a collection of 370lbs of potatoes for the Henley Cottage Hospital. Not a record but our second-best effort.*   1940.2

The village seemed to be awash with activities in aid of the War effort. The WI offered household hints......

> *....Uses for old rubber hot-water bottles - Cut off the edges of old hot-water bottles, and use the circular or oval pieces to put on the bottom of the washing-up bowl. This saves the silver from getting scratched in washing up. The rubber also makes good linings for plate baskets, etc.*

---

[8] On Harpsden Road. In 1919 the Mayor of Henley convened a public meeting to decide on a permanent war memorial and it was decided to build a hospital, which was opened on 3rd June 1923. The hospital was closed in 1985 and subsequently the buildings were demolished.

The harder edges of the bottles make excellent buffers for brooms, carpet-sweepers, etc.

Toys for the bath-tub can also be made; the edges being stuck together with rubber solution. In sticking the edges together leave a small space for inflating before finally sealing.

To clean linoleum - In wet weather when the kitchen linoleum gets extra dirty, a good plan is to sprinkle some paraffin on a wad of newspaper and rub the floor over with this, to remove the mud stains. It can then be polished in the, ordinary way, as the paraffin dries immediately, and is better for the linoleum than water. 1940.2

A 'Hambleden Work Party' would meet at Yewden Manor…..

….We have worked for the Bucks Red Cross, the Finnish Red Cross, the Newfoundland War Comforts Committee, the Daily Sketch War Comforts Fund and Mine-sweepers. Up to date our output has been — 110 helmets, 25 pairs pants, 20 day shirts, 25 nightshirts, 33 hot bottle covers, 136 floor cloths, 48 pairs bed socks, 49 bedjackets, 15 helpless case shirts, 80 Dorothy bags, 53 pairs mittens, 6 pairs gum boot stockings, 3 pairs gloves, 4 pairs Minesweepers gloves, 2 pullovers, 8 pairs cuffs, 52 scarves, 198 many-tailed bandages and 4,290 swabs. In all 757 garments and 4,290 surgical swabs. 1940.3

…..The Work Party reached its first anniversary on May 22nd. The work sent away during that time numbers 5,480, which includes

4,290 surgical swabs. Work has been sent out to the British Red Cross, Finnish Red Cross, Newfoundland War Comforts Fund, Daily Sketch, Oxford & Bucks Regiment, Deep Sea Mission and Lady Smith Dorrien[9]. Details are - 125 helmets, 96 scarves, 59 mittens, 96 pair socks, 22 sea boot stockings, 12 pullovers, 16 cuffs, 13 minesweeping gloves, 6 knitted gloves, 10 flannel shirts, 62 bedjackets, 2 waistcoats, 25 pants, 20 day shirts, 45 hut bottle covers, 136 floor cloths, 49 bed socks, 15 helpless case shirts[10], 181 many tail bandages[11], 11 pyjama suits, 178 ditty' bags[12], 4290 surgical swabs. 1940.6

....H.R.H. The Duchess of Kent visited the work room on February 5th 1942.3

It seems that people not only worked hard, but also dug deep into their pockets in aid of the War effort.

On Whitsun, the children of the Sunday Schools had traditionally collected farthings for charity. In 1944 they collected the truly astonishing number of

---

[9] During the Great War Lady Smith-Dorrien founded the Lady Smith-Dorrien's Hospital Bag Fund. After hearing in April 1915 that it was hard to safeguard wounded soldiers' valuables while they were in hospitals, she wrote to her husband, offering to sew bags for soldiers to hold their valuables in. The Fund reopened in 1940.

[10] The 'helpless case shirt' was designed especially for people with arm injuries. The pattern was created so that the shirt was reversible, meaning it could be worn by patients with injuries on either the right or left arm. One arm of the shirt was finished like a normal bed shirt; however, the other was left open and had tapes to fasten it closed, around the injured arm.

[11] A many-tailed bandage is a bandage or binder with split ends that's used on the trunk and limbs.

[12] A small bag used to carry one's personal effects or toiletries while traveling

11,493 farthings - which works out to be £11/19/5¼. Remember in 1940 £1 was the equivalent of £70 today![13]

The Christmas Day collection in 1940 raised a record £22/10/0 for the Waifs and Strays Society. Carol singers in 1941 raised £24 for St. Dunstan's and the Russian Red Cross Fund. The Red Cross Whist Drive held before Christmas resulted in the raising of the sum of over £14 which meant that 10/- was sent to every local man serving in H.M. Forces. The Red Cross also collected pennies towards a 'rural pennies fund'. In August 1942 they had collected a grand total of £56/10/5 since the Fund was started in March.

Such donations were well appreciated. Two letters to the parish are of note....

> ....You know how missionaries have succoured the wounded, have helped our refugees, and have faced the bayonets, cannons and bombs, and have stood their ground. The Generalissimo and I feel that no words which we could speak could sufficiently express our debt of gratitude to the missionary body, all over China, who have been a help to the distressed and the best of friends to the hundreds of thousands of refugees
>
> Madame Chang Kai Shek.   1943.2
>
> ......Dear Rector

_____

[13] I imagine some poor devil in the bank had to count them!

I am delighted to hear from the Red Cross and the St. John War Organisation that you have forwarded such a splendid donation for my 'Aid to Russia' Fund as the result of two Whist Drives and Dances organised by you and your Committee at Greenlands and Hambleden.

The demands on the resources are increasing daily, and, although it has now reached £2,750,000, we find great difficulty in covering the cost of all the supplies that are needed, and every contribution is more than ever welcome. I shall be grateful if you will convey my most sincere thanks to all those who helped in any way to raise the generous sum of £170/18/6 which, you may rest assured, will be used to the best possible advantage for the alleviation of suffering among the Russian people.

Yours sincerely,

Clementine S. Churchill,   10, Downing Street, Whitehall, 29th March 1943   1943.5

Apart from raising money and making items for the Red Cross, the War affected the village in other ways…..

….Owing to the lighting regulations, we have been forced to alter the time of our Evening services. After much thought, it has been decided to overcome the difficulty by holding the Evening Services at 3 p.m.   1939.10

.....In the event of sirens being sounded during the hours of Divine Worship, the following action will be taken in all three Churches of the Parish. At the first appropriate moment there will be a pause in the Service for three minutes during which the organ will play some well-known hymns. During this three minutes' interlude those who have to report for duty will leave the Church. The rest of the congregation can remain in their places if they so desire. Immediately after the three minutes' interlude the Service will continue. In the event of an air raid actually taking place during Divine Worship, members of the congregation are expected to put their trust in God, to remain quietly in their places, and to follow the lead given by their clergy. The above instructions apply to Services other than the Service of Holy Communion. The Service of Holy Communion will not be interrupted unless absolutely necessary. Those who have to report for duty are asked to do so as quietly as possible. 1939.11

The Parish Magazine did not record the awful air crash up at Fawley, though all must have known about it – perhaps even heard it or saw the fireball and smoke above the trees on the horizon. It was the worst disaster experienced locally.

On 14th March 1943, Halifax DG283 of 161 Squadron suffered engine failure and crashed at Last Cottage in Fawley. The pilot was 21-year-old Flying Officer Geoffrey Osborn. The flight had taken off from RAF Tempsford (Bedfordshire) for a secret night-time Special Operations Executive mission to drop supplies to the Resistance near the Swiss border in France, a near

1,000-mile round trip. Its cargo included fifteen crates of homing pigeons. On crashing, the aircraft, carrying a full load of fuel for this incredibly long journey, skidded down the slope, hit the trees, and burst into flames.

It was the scene of a quite remarkable act of bravery by F/O Osborne, as described in his citation for the George Medal:

Flying Officer Geoffrey Osborn

> *In March, 1943, Flying Officer Osborn was captain and pilot of an aircraft which crashed shortly after taking off on an operational flight. The aircraft was soon enveloped in flames and ammunition and verey lights were exploding. Flying Officer Osborn was dazed but succeeded in extricating five injured members of the crew from the wreckage. In so doing he was badly burnt about the hands, arms and face. Though in a state bordering on collapse, he did all he could to ensure that every member of his crew had been extricated before he was finally persuaded to receive attention.*

His decoration was personally awarded by the King.

The members of his crew were:
F/O D Thornton – Navigator
F/Sgt Stevens - Air Gunner

Sgt R Poltock – Flight Engineer

Sgt H Shearer – Wireless Operator

Sgt B Crane – Air Gunner

Sadly, Sergeants Crane and Shearer succumbed to their injuries two days later.

No-one one knows what happened to the pigeons.

Chapter 3

Persons of Significance

With transport being so limited, the village was to a large extent self-sufficient at the outbreak of the War. There was a butcher (Bill Wheeler) and a baker/grocer (Mr Saxby), but no mention of a candlestick maker, though wood turning and bodging[14] continued in the woods well into the 1930s. It  had its own school (Headmaster Harold 'Gaffer' Heath), a builders' merchant and coffin maker (Alfred Courtney), a post office, stores and telephone exchange (Arthur Webb). It boasted a village policeman (PC Arthur Tew), a saddler/boot repairer (John Harris). And, of course, a pub, The Stag & Huntsman (George Gloyne, MA Oxon) – see photo. Daily buses from Wycombe to Henley ran through the village.

George Gloyne would have been an interesting man to chat with. Having lived in Java for many years, he must have seemed quite exotic to his customers, few of whom had ever been further afield than Henley. He had been an original member of a Commission elected by the British community at Batavia (modern day Jakata) to find the burial place of the British soldiers who were killed at the, long forgotten, Battle of Cornelis in the Dutch East Indies in 1811, during the Napoleonic Wars. He had spent a considerable time exploring the old battlefield and had carried out some work of

---

[14] Making chair legs, often in a workshop in the woods.

excavation, but without success. In a letter to the Times he recorded that *The battle of Cornelis was one of the most gallant and decisive victories of our Army.* [15]

There were two doctors in the village, Dr John Elliot who lived at Spennythorne, where he had his surgery, and Dr Andrew Wilson who had a surgery in Vine Street (running between the village square and the blacksmith), so called because vines used to grow up the front of the houses[16]. Apparently, they produced grapes, but they were too bitter to eat.

VINE STREET. THE DOCTOR'S SURGERY WAS DOWN THE ARCHWAY ON THE RIGHT – NOW BRICKED UP. THE PRIVIES WERE ON THE LEFT.

Vine Street was also the location of a row of privies for the cottages in the Street. The doctor was one of the few people to own a car (similar to the one in the photo) and was not restricted by petrol rations. His car, though, did have to have headlight hoods in case he was called out at night-time.

---

[15] Letter to the Times 18 March 1939

[16] According to Jim Tilbury – but there doesn't seem to be any trace of them in this 1937 photo.

The old doctor, Dr Wilson, came out of retirement for the War. He lived at Little Colstrope where he reared rainbow trout in the brook that ran through his garden. Although he tried to contain them with a grill, some of the spry  escaped and grew to some size, perhaps 3-4lbs. This photo shows Jim Tilbury (with the rod) and Reg Skates fishing for them in 1942 in the brook in front of the bakery. The old doctor would sometimes join them. He would lie on his stomach in the drying ground[17] behind the smithy, and tickle the trout. When done properly, the fish would go into a trance after a minute or so, and could be easily retrieved. He would either throw them back or give them to Will Lane who worked in the blacksmiths for JT's father, Sid.

Sid Tilbury was one of the few residents of the village that owned a car – a  maroon Wolseley Hornet (similar to the one in the image). Its number was ABH570. It spent most of the War up on blocks because of petrol rationing. About once a month, Sid would crank it up (the battery was flat) and let it run for an hour or so. Perhaps he would and run it round the village, to keep it 'ticking over' as he said.

---

[17] Where villagers hung out their washing to dry.

The blacksmith workshop was across the road from the Tilbury's house, 'The Forge'. (where Webbs, the builders are today). Life for a blacksmith was hard. Sid would set/mould the first batch of bread across the road at the bakery at 4am before he went to work to shoe cart

horses. And if those cart horses happened to be at a distant farm, such as Bockmer End, he would walk up there, about two miles, with eight large, heavy horse shoes and his tool bag. Many farms had their own smithy. Up to and during the War there were 120 farm horses to keep shod. Tractors started coming over from the US after the War.

As well as shoeing horses, Sid was also the village's wheelwright. The making of a cartwheel is a work of art. It is made of three different woods – elm, which has a close grain and rarely splits, for the stock, split oak for the spokes and ash for the rim. Once the pieces are put together, the wheel is laid perfectly flat upon a stand. The red-hot metal tyre is then lifted and quickly laid over the wheel. As the rim falls into position round the circumference of the wheel, water is poured over, cooling it and shrinking it to grip the wood. Though extremely simple, it requires a good deal of team work and experience – too much contraction and the wheel may buckle, too little and it would be too loose. The whole process barely takes three minutes and permits no correction if there is a slip.

The village was fortunate in having its own flour mill (at Mill End) and bakery (see photo) ....

....*The Saxby's had the bakery[18]. I used to work there, cleaning the very large dough machine. I was particularly fond of the lovely sticky buns - Hilda (their daughter) would bring one out with a cuppa.*

Tuppence halfpenny for a loaf in those days (2.5d). Bread was baked all the way through the war.

Owen Webb[19], whose family had the post office, would drive the delivery van on the bread round – 2 or 3 times a week. They would go down to Mill End, along Ferry Lane and then across the river on the chain ferry to go over to Aston delivering bread. They also delivered around the villages.

Ted Daniel owned the mill at Mill End. Tom Thatcher was the lorry driver and had a Foden steam lorry and Bert Wright helped.

---

[18] Saxby's were the tenants of the business owners, Barksfield Brothers - see advertisement on the back cover.

[19] Owen was killed in the War. His name is on the War Memorial.

Grain went to the mill, made into flour, then once full, the four-wheel trailer would go round the blacksmiths shop, over the bridge and reverse it into the bakery. Mrs Hobbs would stand out the front of her house on the corner with her hands wrapped in an apron, daring Tom to go over the triangle of grass. He'd go to London once a fortnight with three or four tons of flour.   JT

A word about the village post office (see photo). Its truly formidable list of duties included....

....Each week 90 old age pensioners draw their dues as honoured beneficiaries of a Democratic State[20]. Each week a sum nearing £90 is paid as separation or family allowances to relations of men and women serving in the armed forces. Government payments for billeting[21] pass over this benevolent counter each week to deserving recipients. The War Savings of the village are deposited here, and during the 'Salute the Soldier' week, a total of £2,300 was received. Postal drafts of money from relations to serving men and women are forwarded. Money

---

[20] The Widows, Orphans and Old Age Contributory Pensions Act was passed in 1925, establishing a contributory pension for manual workers and others earning up to £250 per year. The pension was paid weekly, with a rate of ten shillings from age 65.

[21] The billeter received 10s. 6d. From the government for taking a child. Another 8s. 6d. per head was paid if the billeter took more than one. For mothers and infants, the billeter provided lodging only at a cost of 5s. per adult and 3s. per child.

Orders and Postal Orders are issued, and, of course, ubiquitous stamps of all values. The Post Office Savings Bank with its beneficent convenience is fully operated here. Telegrams are received and delivered to a wide area. Dog, gun and wireless licences are issued. A telephone kiosk is also available. The establishment is the clearing centre of Village War Emergency Services.[22]

An essential, but unsung, member of the community was Dyker Hobbs. Most houses (and the school[23]) in Hambleden had outside lavatories which had to be emptied on a regular basis.....

A Modern photo of the Vine Street privies

....my pal, Stan Hobbs used to live up at Coombe Terrace. His Dad was Dyker[24] Hobbs as he used to have to empty the night soil from their outside toilets (at night). It was taken to the back of the timber yard where there was a great barrel. Someone from the timber yard got a tractor and would take the barrel to where the car park is at Mill End, where there was a pit[25], and the contents of the barrel were

---

[22] Thomas B Scotcher : An English Village in War-Time (writing about Binfield Heath – but there is no reason to suppose that Hambleden was any different).

[23] Dyker Hobbs was still emptying the school lavatories well into the 1950s.

[24] Outside privies were called dykes.

[25] Left from the excavations of the Roman villa by Alfred Cox in 1912.

> *emptied into it. The barrel worked on a chain with a winch to tip it (used to be pulled by horses but later by tractor).*   JT

An interesting member of the community was King Zog of the Albanians. He had been forced from power by Mussolini in 1939, and in 1941 moved his court to the country house of Parmoor[26] in Frieth, of all places. His retainers lived in Little Parmoor.

The king and his Hungarian wife were an exotic couple – Geraldine beautiful and glamorous, Zog described as 'the last ruler of romance', one of the 'cleverest men in Europe' and 'frankly, a cad'. He kept gold coins in chests in the hall at Parmoor and reputedly smoked 200 cigarettes a day.

He did not always treat the house with respect, as a quote from the period shows:

> *"To the consternation of the guests, King Zog's goat, which lived in the house, strayed into the dining room during a dinner party and proceeded to eat the tablecloth, causing all the dishes to crash to the floor".[27]*

---

[26] Parmoor had been the house of Charles Cripps, 1st Baron Parmoor. His son, Stafford, served in the 1945-1951 Attlee ministry, first as President of the Board of Trade and between 1947 and 1950 as Chancellor of the Exchequer. Stafford was also part of Churchill's wartime ministry, went on a special wartime mission to the Soviet Union, and was considered – or considered himself – a possible replacement for Churchill as wartime leader.

[27] https://www.chilterns.org.uk/map_marker/king-zog-of-albania/

THE ALBANIAN ROYAL FAMILY AT PARMOOR.

His wife, Geraldine, played an active role in village affairs....

....H.M. Queen Geraldine of the Albanians gave a delightful children's party to over 100 children in the Village Hall. The children were delighted that Her Majesty graciously came herself. They were all sorry that H.H. the Crown Prince could not be present. 1942.2

....Her Majesty, Queen Geraldine of the Albanians declared the Red Cross fete open. 1942.9

Although it was to Rector Watts that villagers turned for guidance, both spiritual and secular, the lord of the manor was William Henry 'Billy' Smith, 3rd Viscount Hambleden, chairman of the stationers WH Smith (hereafter referred to as Lord Hambleden).

Although the Elizabethan Manor House had been in his family since 1871, Lord Hambleden and his family chose to live at Greenlands House[28], a

---

[28] Greenlands was the home of Lord and Lady Hambleden until 1946, when they moved from there into Hambleden Manor House. Greenlands became Henley Management College, now a part of Reading University. It was dressed in camouflage during the War.

palatial riverside mansion. The Manor House had been leased to Mrs Eleanor Stainton since 1924, and would continue to be so until 1945, when Lord  Hambleden transferred his residence there. Billy did not enjoy the Manor House for long, dying after a short illness in 1948 aged only 44; he was much mourned.

Incidentally, the death duties were so severe that his shareholding in WH Smith was sold to staff and the public, and the company that had been owned by the Smith family since 1792 became publicly owned.

Most of the villagers either owed their livelihood or their house, often both, to the Estate. Until quite recently male members of the community would doff their caps or touch their forelocks as Lord or Lady Hambleden drove or rode past. Most local disputes were resolved jointly by Lord Hambleden and Rector Watts. It was, to a large extent, still a feudal village, and would remain (decreasingly) so until the 4th Lord Hambleden emigrated to America in 1988. Much of the Estate was sold in 2007.

In 1938, Lord Hambleden had purchased the house we now know as Kenricks from the diocese. Up to that time it had been the Rectory. In that year a new residence for the Rector was built further up the hill above the former rectory, which now needed a new name. Eventually 'Kenricks' was

_____

decided upon, honouring the Georgian renovator of the old manor house. Lord Hambleden chose not to use Kenricks as a family residence but proceeded to let it out

The first tenant was Rt Hon Edward Algernon FitzRoy MP, Speaker of the House of Commons. He had taken Kenricks on a 14-year lease from Lord Hambleden as a country retreat away from Westminster. Already in his early seventies when living at Kenricks, Speaker FitzRoy contracted pneumonia and did not live out the length of his lease; he died at Speaker's House, Westminster, on 3 March 1943. The customary retirement honour for Speakers was awarded to his widow, Muriel, who became Viscountess Daventry. She was still at Kenricks in 1945, but moved soon after the War.

On 12 May 1940, while at Kenricks, FitzRoy wrote to Neville Chamberlain regretting the criticism of Chamberlain in the House of Commons and in appreciation of his broadcast following his resignation as Prime Minister[29]. We are unable to ascertain how widely his views were held in the village.

When Kenricks was vacated by Viscountess Daventry, it proved the perfect place to offer to Mrs Stainton, widowed since 1927, and she moved there from the Manor House with her unmarried daughter Catherine. They would continue to live there until Mrs Stainton's death in 1955.

In 1937, when the new Queen Elizabeth (later the Queen Mother) had need to enlarge her Household, she invited Patricia Hambleden to be a Lady of the Bedchamber. At first Lady Hambleden declined, afraid that royal duties

---

[29] University of Birmingham, Cadbury Research Library ref NC7/11/33/66

would interfere with her family life (she was to have three sons and two daughters), but when the Queen promised that she would not be called upon during school holidays, she agreed, remaining with the Queen Mother for the rest of her life. She was described as 'a saint, intelligent and humorous, without an ounce of snobbery in her veins'. She died in 1994, aged 89 and a widow for 46 years.

In early 1940, a group of over 30 ladies from a 'well known cripples' home' in Love Walk, Denmark Hill, London took up accommodation at Greenlands for the duration of the War. Part of the drawing room was made into a sitting room and a chapel for them. Rector Watts visited regularly to take Holy Communion and found the ladies 'very delightful'. Members of Greenlands Hostel held a Christmas carol party in 1943, and raised £13/5/6 for the Red Cross. By the time they returned to London in July 1945, they had become a bit of a fixture in the village; the Rector reflected that…

> ….there will be many sad hearts at their departure. They have endeared themselves to us all, and we shall never forget them.

Greenlands played host to boys from Slough…..

> ….The Boys' Brigade from Slough and Maidenhead will be camping at Greenlands from August 2nd – 16th, by kind invitation of Lord Hambleden. We wish the boys a rollicking good time, although I understand that it is not going to be all play and no work, and that in the mornings they will be helping in the harvesting. Good luck to them. 1941.8

A large, well-appointed house called 'Hambleden Cottage', to distinguish it from Hambleden House, was taken over by an eclectic group.......

.....Several companies brought their registered offices to The Cottage[30]. Among them was the Anglo Burma Tin Company, Apex (Trinidad) Oilfields Ltd., The Anglo-French Exploration Company and Geever Tin Mines Ltd. Quite a few men worked at The Cottage, which in a way, made up for the number of men from Hambleden who had left to join the services. CG

---

[30] It had been the home of the Ryder family in the mid nineteenth century – see my biography of Admiral Sir Alfred Ryder 'To be a Pilgrim'.

Chapter 4

Food and Rationing

Rationing had been introduced in January 1940.

Everyone was issued with a ration book and you always took it to Hambleden Stores and elsewhere to make purchases of rationed items. There was a ration book for clothing, a ration book for food. There was even a ration book for children that regulated the amount of milk which could be purchased for a child. Sugar, bacon, cheese, fats, tea, eggs, meat and sweets were all rationed. Each book was marked out for the whole year with weekly squares. These were referred to as coupons. The coupons certainly didn't guarantee that you could buy commodities. If the goods were available, the shopkeeper (Mr Saxby) sold you your allowance eg two ounces of butter per person per week. He then took or cancelled your coupons.

If supplies of something needed were seen being delivered to Hambleden Stores, a queue quickly formed. If you were early in the queue you might be lucky. It was all part of daily life. Shortages, of course, led to the black market. Things were said to be available 'under the counter'.

Many locals were still keeping pigs in their back yards and you were allowed to kill them for food. However, the Ministry for Food would greatly reduce your meat ration for a whole year because of this. We didn't barter food; we shared what we had.

Of course, we all kept chickens for the supply of eggs and cockerels were fattened up for Christmas. Rabbits were snared and the odd pheasant or two might be unlucky enough to stray into your garden![31]   CG

Amounts of basic foods such as meat, cheese and sugar were set for adults regardless of age, gender, class or occupation. At the beginning only bacon, butter, and sugar were rationed, with meat, cheese and tea later added to the list. Most food rations were allocated by weight, but meat by price. Allocated rations varied throughout the war depending on supply levels.

Pregnant and nursing mothers were given additional allowances of food such as meat to sustain them. Children and babies also had different rations including extra milk and meat, as well as the provision of orange juice and cod liver oil.

Free school milk was supplied to the school. At the start of the War, it was delivered in milk crates containing small bottles and was always left in the playground. In the winter, the bottles were often frozen, and the milk expanded and forced off the cardboard top. The bottles were then arranged near the open fire to thaw out, leaving the children with the unforgettable taste of lukewarm milk. By contrast, in the summer, the crates were left in the sun and by the time the children were given the milk, it was 'on the turn'.

---

[31] Charles forgot to mention that beekeeping came back into its own.

Later in the War, owing to the scarcity of glass for making the bottles, the milk was delivered in churns. The children were provided with beakers, and the milk was doled out by the teachers and senior pupils.

The milk was of varying quality and had to be tested by county inspectors on a regular basis. At other times, there was simply not enough milk available for the free milk allocation. On 9 December 1940, the headmaster reported that the.......

> ....supply of milk to the children resumed today after a lapse of a month, during which supply has been insufficient.

Everyone was issued with a coloured ration book according to their status. People were required to register with shops, and when purchasing food, they presented their ration book for verification of the amounts allocated to them.

Married women bore the brunt of having to adjust to the ration system because they were primarily responsible for feeding family members. These women pooled the quantities of food allocated to each member of their family, allowing their households to benefit. Some mothers used children's extra meat ration to feed larger portions to fathers, while also using the children's orange juice allowance in their cookery dishes. The Parish Magazine carried ration-based recipes, such as:

> *A cake made without eggs.*
>
> *Ingredients : 6 oz. self-raising flour, 2 oz. rice flour (or ground rice), 4 oz. sugar, 4 oz. fat, 4 oz. fruit (sultanas or raisins), 1*

dessertspoon vinegar, 1 gill of milk, 1 teaspoon of bicarbonate of soda, pinch of salt.

Method : Sift the flour, sugar, and salt together, rub in the fat, and then mix in the fruit. Put the bicarbonate of soda into the milk warmed. Stir well and add the vinegar to it. Mix this with dry ingredients and bake for one and a half hours in a moderate oven.   *1940.2*

The landlord of the Stag and Huntsman, George Gloyne, offered his own contribution...

.....Yesterday I asked one of the villagers to gather from the hedgerows a bundle of wild hop shoots. I served them up undisguised as a course for dinner. Not one guest refused the course and all declared them to be a worthy substitute for asparagus. Not one plate was returned to the kitchen. That course cost me a 5d. pint of beer![32]

In 1941, the government introduced a points-based scheme for certain items including tinned goods. Hambleden School shared in the distribution of these new points ration books, and more than 700 were distributed at the school in December. Shoppers had the freedom to apply their allocated points to purchase foods covered under this system, which allowed more

---

[32] Letter to the Times 30 April 1940

flexibility in the food programme and gave consumers more choice in constructing their meals.

During the war, foods such as SPAM and powdered eggs were shipped from America to Britain through the Lend-Lease Agreement between the two countries. Spam is a portmanteau of "spiced ham" and, developed in 1937, became popular warfare food for the ration-starved folk owing to its long shelf life. It was mocked for its gristly taste and general awfulness and, as we all know, has since become a byword for unwanted emails.

Margarine, which was largely disliked before the war, became a part of the rations allotted to each household, but remained unpopular.

Many potatoes were used by the Pig Club....

.....Bowdens in Yewden Farm grew potatoes for the Pig Club. They would be lifted and stained with gentian violet so you couldn't use them in the food chain, and then distributed when wanted to the pig club. The potatoes were mixed with the swill from Greenlands and RAF Danesfield and boiled up in a copper or wash boiler/oil drum . You had to make sure there were no knives, forks and spoons in the swill - if there were you'd send them back.   JT

Pigs were a staple in the village. JT remembers....

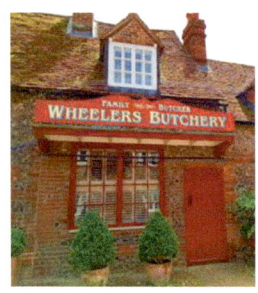
Bill Wheeler ran the butchers, which was owned by William Lees who also owned one in Wallingford and one in Bell St, Henley. They had a farm at the top of White Hill in Henley where livestock were reared. Hambleden had a Pig Club because most of the households kept pigs. We had two, which were kept in the stable at the back of the blacksmith's shop. Everyone down the workhouse yard (now the allotments by the south bridge) had pigsties. Ted Belton (head forester) had a pigsty. Bill Wheeler would do the slaughtering when the time was right. You gave up your meat ration coupons but you kept one pig. The other pig went into the Ministry. No restriction on the size of the pig.

Danny Daniels was the manager of the mill at Mill End and there were always toppings (part of the waste) and bran which you could buy at knock down prices. That would bring your pigs on to a good size and Bill would do the butchering on a Sunday morning there and then, either on site or in the slaughterhouse at the bottom of the yard behind his shop.

The method was to get a bale of straw, knock the pig out then cut its throat and bleed it (hang it round the back), then lay it out on the bale of straw, and burn all the hair off, roll it on its back and split it down middle, and put the entrails out into an old bath. I remember seeing my mum with a length of cane getting the entrails out, making chitterlings (small intestines of the pig).

I remember the Landrace pig which had a long body and one extra rib. Our pigs were Large White (long snout) and Middle White (nose turned up), and Landrace pigs. Piglets came from David Keene (Senior) who bred pigs on his farm at Colstrope.

Sides of bacon were salted. Some houses still have rings in the ceiling where the sides of bacon were hung.

Arther Wheeler took over the butchery from his brother after the War. Here he is on his 100th birthday party with Lady Hambleden and the author.

Charles Gray remembered the land army girls[33] fondly.....

........They worked on farms replacing farm labourers and young farmers who had gone into the services. Not all young men on farms went away as farming was a reserved occupation.

As the Land Army was not a military force, uniform was not compulsory. However, if they chose, land girl volunteers were issued with the following on signing up:

---

[33] JT thinks they were accommodated in the Manor Houe,

- 2 green jerseys
- 2 pairs of breeches
- 2 overall coats
- 2 pairs of dungarees
- 6 pairs of thick stockings
- 3 shirts
- 1 overcoat
- 1 pair of stout shoes
- 1 pair of gumboots
- Green Women's Land Army armlet
- Women's Land Army metal badge

They were left in no doubt that items of uniform had to be looked after with great care and could only be replaced after six months, and only then if they were worn out.

Women not only worked on farms; some were in the Timber Corps……

….My sisters, Margaret and Flo Tilbury were timber jills (lumberjills). On the estate they were cutting fir poles for pit props and all up Pheasants Hill farm where Alfie Austin used to live. The trees were felled, then they would get a hoe and debark them.

Some girls stayed in Fingest House; others stayed in the Manor House. They had entertainment evenings, when they would party with the RAF chaps from Danesfield. There were rumours of high jinks!

Sister Flo went to the Warren Row factory which was making fuel pumps for spitfires and worked there. An underground factory - go along the Wargrave road, before Marsh Mill. The drive on the left used to go into the underground factory. JT

In spite of all the hardships, life in Hambleden carried on much as usual. 'Dig for Victory' was the slogan of the time. Every garden and allotment grew as much as possible and of course all the local farmers were working at full strength to produce food. CG

Chapter 5

Children, Evacuees & the School

Fear that German bombing would cause civilian deaths prompted the government to evacuate children, mothers with infants and the infirm from British towns and cities during the War. Evacuation was voluntary, but the fear of bombing, the closure of many urban schools and the organised transportation of school groups helped persuade families to send their children away to live with strangers.

Parents were issued with a list detailing what their children should take with them when evacuated. These items included a gas mask in a case, a change of underclothes, night clothes, plimsolls (or slippers), spare stockings or socks, toothbrush, comb, towel, soap, face cloth, handkerchiefs and a warm coat. Many families struggled to provide their children with all of the items listed.

Practice drills had taken place throughout August 1939. Children would meet at school and walk to pre-arranged departure points at bus stops and stations. On 31 August 1939, announcements were made via radio, newspapers and telegrams that Operation Pied Piper would begin the next day. It would be the biggest and most concentrated mass movement of people in Britain's history. In the first four days of September 1939, nearly 1,500,000 people were transported from towns and cities thought to be in danger from enemy bombers to places of safety in the countryside, such as Hambleden. By any measure it was an astonishing event, a logistical nightmare of co-ordination and control.

27 child evacuees arrived in Hambleden on 12 September 1939, only some nine days after war was declared. By the end of the year, a total of 54 children had arrived, more or less on a weekly basis. They had left busy train stations, shouting officials and sobbing mothers instructing their children: 'Don't complain,' 'Grin and bear it,' 'Look after your sister,' 'Write home as soon as you can.' It was like going on an adventure.

Like many villages, Hambleden was barely ready for the influx. Whereas the departure of the children from the areas thought to be most at risk went relatively smoothly, the same cannot be said of their reception at their destination. The Government had left responsibility for the children's arrival and care to local authorities, with little more than an injunction to do their best. The result can only be described as a typical British wartime shambles. Hundreds of children arrived in the wrong area with insufficient rations. And, more worryingly, there were not enough homes in which to put them. Twelve months earlier, the Government had surveyed available housing, but what they had not taken into account was the extent to which middle-class and well-to-do families would be making their own private arrangements. Consequently, those households who had previously offered to take in evacuees were now full.

The allocation of children to their new homes was made according to rudimentary principles. Billeting officers simply lined the children up against a wall in the village hall, and invited potential hosts to take their pick!

By the end of 1939, when the widely expected bombing raids on cities had failed to materialise, many parents whose children had been evacuated in September decided to bring them home again. By December, 13 had returned to their homes from Hambleden.

Further rounds of evacuation occurred in the summer and autumn of 1940, following the German invasion of France in May-June and the beginning of the Blitz in September. By the end of the War 128 youngsters had been housed and schooled in the village. Some did not stay long; the average length of stay was ten months, though this encompasses a spread of between 2 days and 30 months. Some had to leave when they reached the school leaving age of fourteen. A few did not return home until after the War had ended.

They were transferred to an environment they likely found strange, perhaps hostile[34] in some cases, and had to start a new life with different 'parents' and go to a new school. Evacuees and their hosts were often astonished to

---

[34] 10-year-old Philip Cook remembered regular pitched battles with the Cockney evacuees. (https://www.henleystandard.co.uk/news/community/96521/philip-cook-april-25-1930-to-december-16-2015.html

see how each other lived. Most evacuees flourished in their new surroundings. They would remember their days in Hambleden as the best of times - a life-enhancing, mind-broadening experience, leaving them with memories they treasure to this day. Jim Tilbury remembered after eighty years that '*They all mixed in ok*'. But there must have been those, the minority, to whom it would be the worst of times as they endured a dark and troubled time away from home. They had no idea when they might be going home, if ever. Many evacuees from inner-city areas had never seen farm animals before or eaten vegetables. In many instances a child's upbringing in urban poverty was misinterpreted as parental neglect.

Many children came in groups of three or four from a particular school; most came from west London, Hammersmith in particular. At least they had a few familiar faces around them. Sadly, a few came as singletons. One poor six-year-old arrived on his own from Scotland, a lone seven-year-old arrived from Liverpool. and an eight-year-old from Newcastle. Whereas every evacuee had his or her individual tale to tell, one may only imagine at the despair of such singletons who were placed in a strange land that had fields, woods and livestock, and where the natives spoke in accents different to theirs. Life must have been wretched for them.

Each little evacuee, some as young as 4, had to be billeted. Some would have had happy homes, some perhaps less so. The school Admission Register identifies that Lord and Lady Hambleden at Greenlands took in 12 souls, but otherwise the Register simply refers to their billets as 'Hambleden' or 'Fawley', or 'Pheasants Hill' etc.

Many young children came to Hambleden from London as evacuees. Everyone who had a spare room in their house took children in. The young evacuees almost doubled the number of children attending Hambleden school.   *CG*

Evacuees Bimbo O'Donald lodged at Hatchman's and Barry Grossmith was with the Courtneys in the village. Two were at Mrs. Creed's, one at Edith Austin's. June and Daphne Milland lodged with Mr & Mrs Shannon, and Pat and Barbara Stewart stayed with us at The Forge. I remember Mrs. Stewart, Barbara and Pat's mum, came to see them. She brought with her a piece of bomb shrapnel that was stuck in their front door in their house in London after an air raid. On it was engraved the same number of their house!   *JT*

Evelyn Robinson remembers….

….I was 9 when the war broke out in September. It was announced that we are at war with Germany so we rushed out into the garden in Hayes (Kent), then suddenly the sirens went so we all rushed back but the all clear was then soon sounded.

I was evacuated to relatives in Turville in 1940, as living 3 miles from Biggin Hill, there was a lot of aircraft activity (bombers, fighters etc) during the Battle of Britain. I was there for about 9 weeks, through the Battle of Britain, and then back to Hayes.

Then the V1 rockets started in 1944. Before then you could feel safe during the day but no longer as they were happening all the time so when my Aunt Fan died in September 1944, my father asked the solicitor in Henley if they could rent the cottage in Turville, which they did.

I worked in the shop in Turville on a Saturday. The shop was next to the pub. After their meal the old chaps would sit out on the green and talk to each other. The evacuees brought new life to the parish.

Christmas was a particularly emotional time for the evacuees,. a time when homesickness and loneliness was at its worst. Lord and Lady Hambleden attempted to provide a bit of cheer by holding Christmas parties at Greenlands. For instance, the Parish Magazine recorded that.....

.....On Friday, December 22nd the annual Christmas Tree Party was given to the Children by Lord and Lady Hambleden. About 160 children sat down to tea — a number of them being evacuees. Judging by the noise the children made, they enjoyed themselves better than ever this year.   1940.1

Evacuees and their hosts were comforted by the radio programme Children's Hour[35], which was broadcast by the BBC from 5 pm to 6 pm every day of the week. Since 1923, the programme had become established as a permanent and popular part of the daily life, with a rapidly growing audience. By the mid-1930s the programme was a national institution, and by 1939, the audience had reached four million. In 1940, the 14-year-old Princess Elizabeth

---

[35] Strictly speaking: 5 pm to 5.55. The last five minutes were assigned to the Weather Forecast

broadcast her best wishes to those children who had been evacuated from Britain to America, Canada and elsewhere. Princess Margaret joined her to wish all children goodnight.

Children's Hour was hosted by 'Uncle Mac[36]' whose signoff line, "Goodnight children, everywhere," became particularly poignant to those children who were away from their homes.

All the evacuees had to attend school. Hambleden School, which was used to accommodating 85 children in two classrooms in peacetime, now had to accommodate up to 176! A master from St Paul's C of E School, Hammersmith was relocated on a semi-permanent basis to help out, and other St Paul's teachers came on occasional days. Locals, possibly retired teachers, assisted from time to time on a temporary basis.

> ....*At the school initially, there was an empty classroom used for storage, but when all the evacuees arrived (there were about 30) they opened it for them. and the upper school was arranged into two classes. A teacher, Mr. Moore, came down from London for the class.* JT

---

[36] Derek McCulloch

It was a difficult time for the Headmaster, Harold Heath. From the comfortable (unimaginative, complacent) existence of running a small country school, with an adjacent headmaster's house provided, at a stoke he had to deal with up to double the number of children, many of whom were unsettled and unhappy. He was under constant scrutiny. He was used to a rather cosy termly visit from the Diocesan Schools Inspector whose chief concern seemed to revolve around standards of religious instruction and worship. However, he received a wakeup call in May 1939 when the school was inspected by the County Education Board's Inspector, a process not unlike that experienced by schools today. His report was not good…

MODERN IMAGE OF THE SCHOOL. THE HEADMASTER'S HOUSE CAN BE SEEN IN THE BACKGROUND

> *There are 85 children on the roll, all of whom are of good type. They are well behaved, neat in appearance, and generally speaking, diligent and industrious.*
>
> *Though some improvement has taken place since the last report in the quality of the written work, there is still room for improvement. The early use of the pen may account for some of the weaknesses in writing and figuring noticeable throughout the school.*
>
> *The unsatisfactory level reached by the oldest scholars in mental arithmetic, as evidenced by the low marks gained in the test worked by Class 1 and by the unreasonable amount of*

marginal work allowed in the notebooks, indicates the necessity for more frequent and systematic practice in quick mental processes.

Much of the written arithmetic is very academic and unreal. The syllabus ought to be revised so as to afford the pupils more opportunities for dealing with problems of everyday experiences.

Generally speaking, the oral reading is fluent. The diction, however, in this subject and in recitation, would be more pleasing if the children were encouraged to speak more deliberately and with attention to correct intonation. In the infants' class some up to date reading books are needed. The composition exercise shows a fair command of vocabulary and idiom. The output of the written exercises might now be increased along the lines suggested during the visit.

Responses in Geography and to a lesser extent in History and Nature Study is disappointing. While the children appear to have some store of facts, the older scholars experienced considerable difficulty in displaying such knowledge by means of oral answers. The School's beautiful environment affords exceptional facilities out of doors for practical observation in connection with all these subjects, and in view of this, the schemes of work should be revised as to make fuller use of such excellent opportunities.

The choral singing possesses some merit. A few representative works by composers other than those found in the National Song Book should be added to the repertory. Sight singing is very weak. A course of instruction should now be planned so as to provide an earlier beginning from staff notation.

A little colour training and weaving has been attempted with some success in Class 2. These might be extended with advantage to Class 1. The older boys received practical instruction in handicraft and the girls attend domestic subjects at 'centres.'[37] This, however, ought not to preclude the adoption of a definite form of craftwork for all the pupils in Classes 1 and 2.

It was clear that the school had to up its game, for very soon, the headmaster not only had to deal with an influx of evacuee children, but also suffer regular visits from London County Council inspectors and the headmistress of St Paul's School. There were also monthly inspections from the county Medical Officer of Health to check for headlice. Serious stuff!

Not only did Mr Heath have to improve the academic curriculum, but he had to consider how to react to the demands of war. In May, 1940 the windows were treated with brown sticky tape criss-crossing the window in a union jack type format to prevent injury from shards of flying glass caused by bomb blast. A month later the school lobbies were converted into splinter proof

---

[37] Senior girls attended weekly domestic science classes in Marlow.

shelters. They were used for the first time on September 5th and at least seven times subsequently (to much merriment from the pupils, I suspect!) In October 1940, air raid warnings had become so frequent that *'to allow us to get some work done, we are trying the spotting system (?) when weather conditions allow.'* In March. 1942 the school was fitted with a set of blackout curtains.[38]

To youngsters at the village school, it was all a bit of fun. To them, it always seemed to be summer. This was how the world was – a world of unspoilt woods and wide streams; they had not known any other.

It was the world of William, Richmal Crompton's[39] scruffy, incorrigible hero who always had well-meant plans that went awry. William had endless optimism – if he wanted something he would find a way to make it happen and when things went wrong, as they always did, he would think of a way, however unconventional, of 'sorting it out'....

> ....*Along Westfield Farm, Medmenham, where there is the new driveway, just inside there was a Nissan hut and it was a practice firing range for the army with anti-tank guns and they used to run exercises using live ammunition. They had something (an old tank?) as a target. US forces used to use it amongst others – they*

---

[38] A bit late in the day?

[39] Richmal Crompton was a hugely popular children's author whose best known books are the William stories (first published in 1922) about a mischievous 11-year-old schoolboy and his band of friends, known as "The Outlaws".

would move in for a week, then another group. The Americans stayed at Phyllis Court.

I remember that Stan Hobbs and one of the evacuees that lived at Pheasants Hill just before the cemetery, Frank Marshall, went on a sortie to Westfield to see what they could find where the target practice had been. They found a mortar bomb so they got it and went up through the woods, across the top to the road which goes up to Rockwell End by the chalk pit and they chucked it away and it went into the road and it exploded. Fortunately, they were behind a tree and it went off behind another so they avoided any of the shrapnel. They got away with it!

We used to dam the stream by the village's north bridge to create a pond for (very cold) swimming. It would flood the nearby field and drive Alfie Austin, the farmer, wild!   JT

The telephone poles were fair game....

....the telephone wires came into Hambleden on telephone poles, with two or three cross bars, four lines per cross bar. The wires were connected to the cross bars by white porcelain cups. These were fair target for us boys with catapults and throwing stones. Hell to pay if we were caught! But that is how we learned to throw a cricket ball from the boundary to the. stumps.   CG

...Along the woods you would see some of the phosphorous flares which were dropped with parachutes but hadn't ignited. A

lot ended up in the trees, and we would go to try and get hold of the silk parachutes which were very popular with the girls!

I picked up a piece of phosphorus as big as a cob nut and took it to school. Gaffer Heath asked what it was. I said I wasn't sure or that's what I said, so the teacher picked it up and threw it in the fire (open fire) and while he was warming himself with his back to the fire the phosphorous ignited and scorched his trousers! PC Tew, the local policeman, came and gave us a talk about picking up strange things in the woods.   *JT*

The risk of an incendiary bomb setting the school on fire was a constant worry in the early years of the War. Consequently, in September 1940 the senior boys were instructed in the use of the stirrup pump by Mr. Partridge, Chief of the Hambleden Auxiliary Fire Service. In September 1941 the school received another stirrup pump and two sand buckets from county HQ in Aylesbury. Boys were employed in their spare time filling sandbags.

Gas masks were issued to all children as a precaution against attack by gas bombs. The masks came in cardboard boxes, with a strap for carrying them on the shoulder. Children were instructed to keep their masks with them at all times and were the key item of luggage for evacuees. They were regularly inspected. Wearing them was just a game to most children. They would cause considerable annoyance by making a 'raspberry' noise every time they breathed out.

As before the War, disease and weather played havoc with school attendances which could not have made maintenance of standards easy:

- Dec 8, 1939 : A very wet morning and a poor attendance.
- Jan 29, 1940 : a very wintry morning with much snow. The attendance is much reduced - only 69 children are present. (out of 113)
- Feb 9, 1940 : Illness and bad weather have reduced the attendance this morning. There are 43 absent out of 117.
- Apr 2, 1940 : There are 118 names on the register. 34 are absent on account of infectious diseases, German measles and chicken pox.
- Jan 20, 1941 : Snowstorms have reduced the attendance this morning. 42 children are absent.
- Feb 12, 1941 : Epidemic sickness of measles and mumps continues to decrease the attendance
- Jan 6, 1942 : A number of children are suffering from colds and the attendance is poor.
- Jan 16, 1942 : A whooping cough epidemic continues to reduce the attendance. 67 only are in attendance out of a total roll call of 100.
- Jan 20, 1942 : Snow fell very heavily during the night. Only 45 children were at school this morning.
- Jan 23, 1942 : Bad weather continues. Whooping cough has reduced the numbers in attendance to 59.
- Feb 2, 1942 : A very heavy fall of snow during the night brought a further reduction in the attendance this morning. 49 children are present.
- Jan 30, 1944 : Severe weather and a heavy fall of snow reduced to attendance considerably. Today there are 41 out of 63 present.
- 1945, May 7 : Measles has increased rapidly over the week and only 43 children are present this morning out of 70. (That's 27 families who would not be enjoying the Victory festivities in the village the following day!)

Interestingly, out of the six winters between 1939 and 1944, four were blighted by snow. In an age when children walked to school, snow presented a real problem. When was the last time Hambleden experienced four snowbound years out of six?

Gardening had become so popular that in 1941 a children's group was established...

> ....*The children have been divided into groups of seven, each group working one plot. It is hoped that this new body which will be known as the 'Hambleden Junior Horticultural Society' will produce vegetables of various types and of good quality worthy of appearing with other exhibits at the Annual Vegetable and Flower Show which will take place, as usual, this year. A prize will be offered for the best allotment and it appears from the keenness of the boys and girls engaged in this work that there will be active competition for the trophy, which will be given to one of the groups engaged in this new and important venture.*
>
> 1941.4

In June 1940, the headmaster was able to report that

> *111 children are assembled and are accounted for as being in the school, at a domestic centre, in the fields or in the gardens.*

In May 1941, double summertime was introduced which meant that, during spring, clocks moved two hours ahead of GMT instead of one. By extending daylight hours in the evening, it meant less fuel was needed to be used on lighting during the day, and there was more daylight to work in the fields. The school opened at 9:30 AM and closed at 4:30 PM. Double summertime ended in 1945.

In the summer holiday of 1942, the school was occupied by Southall Secondary School as a harvest centre. One evacuee from west London remembered…

> …Some of the school staff organised "harvest camps" during the last weeks of the summer holiday when volunteer boys from the fourth, fifth and sixth forms when into the country to help the farmers with the harvest.
>
> Our first camp was at Hambleden, Buckinghamshire. We were hired out to the farmers in the area. We stood sheaves up onto stooks as the corn was cut, loaded onto carts when dry and did any other unskilled work the farmer needed doing to release the men that he did have for the skilled work.
>
> At Hambleden we slept in the village school and had our meals in the village hall. Those of us in the sixth-form were invited to join the fire-watching rota.
>
> Exercise books were provided by the school to each pupil. Because of the shortage of paper, you were not allowed to leave any empty lines. Each book would be inspected closely before a new one would be issued.[40]

---

[40] https://www.bbc.co.uk/history/ww2peopleswar/stories/26/a7229126.shtml

In October, time usually spent in organised games was given to the children to pick rose hips.

The school did its fair share of fund raising. In May 1943, the children collected over £38 for the 'Wings for Victory' week. In 1944 they saved £221 for the National Savings Association. War Scheme. Their charity was not limited to merely raising money. In 1942, 48 Christmas parcels of socks and gloves were sent to ex scholars who were with the forces. And, curiously, fir cones were collected for the Forestry Commission – '60 bushels'[41] in December 1942. And even curiouser, the children were set the task of capturing and killing queen wasps (good luck with that!) In July 1940, 1,213 insects were destroyed, of which Brian Tew, the son of the village bobby, collected 133.

Somehow they muddled through, and by June 1942 events were such that the school was able to revert to its prewar arrangements in terms of staff and classroom numbers.

---

[41] Over 2,000 kg!

Chapter 6

Home Guard

Rural areas were initially considered those most vulnerable to parachute attack, so Hambleden had its own Home Guard (HG) platoon, No. 6 Platoon (Hambleden) 4 Bucks Bn, with its HQ in Hughenden, of all places. The unit was affiliated to the Oxfordshire and Buckinghamshire Light Infantry, whose cap badge they wore. The platoon was to look for any possible landings by parachutists, so Turville windmill would have been a very good base, high on

a hill overlooking the Hambleden Valley. They practiced shooting in the quarry up Rotten Row. Although many of the members, as farm workers, would have owned a rifle or shotgun and were good shots, one may imagine the platoon was more like the TV version of Dad's Army than the more 'professional' HG company in Henley. Nonetheless, one contemporary film, *Went the Day Well (1942),* which posited a German invasion attempt defeated by the inhabitants of a typical rural village, was filmed at Turville. Members of the local Home Guard are ambushed and shot dead by the Germans. This photo of the Turville Heath Home Guard is taken from the Picture Post in 1940.

 We have no photos of the Hambleden platoon, but we do have one of that of Frieth (courtesy of FriethHistory.org)

Back Row: Toby Martin, Fred Barksfield, Ernie West, Percy West, Jack Sherwood, Jim Robertson

Seated: Jack Shaw, Darrell Collier, George Sherwin, Ken Hobbs, Ted Barksfield

Second Lieutenant Darrell Collier was not only a member of Frieth Home Guard but also a member of Churchill's Secret Army. Although he was colour blind, he was a crack shot, which brought him to the attention of his superiors. In mid- 1940, he was sent to a centre at Osterley where he was trained in the finer points of guerilla warfare. As a member of the secret army, he would have been expected to go into hiding if there was an invasion, then attack the Germans in hit and run attacks. In total there were only around 3,500 of these secret army members nationwide, but they were to be the country's last-ditch defence. After intense training on how to silently kill someone, he recalled being taken to an underground bunker in a wood between Stokenchurch and Fingest. From there he and one or two others were to sit it out after an invasion, until the Germans arrived in the area. As we know, the Germans didn't make it, so his training and hideout in the woods were never needed.

The Rector made himself somewhat unpopular because he did not want any rifles to be taken into the church by the Home Guard (!) He also refused permission for the church tower to be used as a look out post as it would have made the church into a place of war instead of a place of peace. In any case, he said, when some of the Home Guard ventured to go up the tower, many of them realised it was well beyond their capabilities to reach the top!

There was something of a loss of interest by the HG over the winter of 1940-41. As the threat of an invasion receded, the declining prospects of the thrill of detaining bailed out German airmen led to the commanding officer of the 4th Bucks Battalion to tell his men, '*After all the trouble they take to come over and bail out, it is not right for anyone to totally disregard them.*'!

When the air raid warning was sounded they manned first aid posts and did periods of fire watching. The air raid siren was mounted on the roof of Henley Town Hall. CG tells us that.....

> *...the oscillating wailing tone could be easily heard in Hambleden; in fact, you could have heard it in the village in a thunderstorm! The all-clear was just as loud, but was one continuous note.*

> *At the age of 15, I was a member of the first aid group having been taught first aid in the boy scouts. Our headquarters was in the sports club. I remember one night, when a bomb was dropped nearby, diving under the billiard table for safety. We had little equipment - a telephone and a few domestic first aid kits.*

What would have happened if we had had an emergency, I dread to think.

I would imagine that the only buildings of strategic importance were Fawley Court, the telephone exchange and the flour mill at Mill End which were guarded 24/7, with a vehicle checkpoint at the adjacent junction on the  Henley to Marlow road. The security of Hambleden lock at Mill End was the responsibility of the Upper Thames Patrol. Apart from that, I don't know what soldiering they did, and, like Charles, I shudder to think that it would have been only them that would have prevented panzer divisions from crossing the bridge (see photo) and entering the village.

The platoon seemed to spend a lot of time raising money for good cause and enjoying themselves....

.... The Pantomime presented by the Hambleden Platoon of the Home Guard was a terrific success. At all three performances the Hall was packed and an extra performance had to be given so as to enable those who were turned away at the door to see it. I understand that the proceeds from the show and from a previous Whist Drive for the Merchant Navy Comforts Fund reached the amazing figure of £200. The Home Guard, the producers and artists alike, are to be heartily congratulated. The pantomime itself was excellent, I haven't enjoyed anything of its kind so much for years.   *1943.2*

.....The Hambleden Village Hall was filled to capacity on December 3rd, when the Hambleden Platoon of the Home Guard organised a Whist Drive & Dance to raise funds in aid of the Merchant Navy Comforts Service. It was a most successful event, as a result of which no less than £230 was realised. Officers and men of a Guards' detachment[42] stationed in the neighbourhood took full advantage of this event to spend an enjoyable evening. May I express my sincere thanks to all who have helped and supported the Hambleden Platoon to obtain the total sum of £437/10/0 in twelve months for this excellent cause. *1944.4*

Nonetheless, this report from the WI hints of something a bit more serious...

Business for the day included an appeal for equipment for the Home Guard Casualty Stations being set up in the neighbourhood. *1942.4*

---

[42] Royal Engineers at Couch Field Barn.

Chapter 7

Entertainment – radio, cinema and dances

Radio was the most popular form of entertainment during the War, even though enabling it to work was not simple, as Evelyn Robinson explained in Chapter 1. Not only did programmes provide the nation, even the remoter villages such as Hambleden, with a form of escape from the hardships of wartime life, but it was equally important to those serving in the forces, both in Britain and overseas. It was the chief form of news and entertainment, and listening increased during wartime. By 1945 there were nearly ten million radio licences in Britain. Sales of the Radio Times increased during the War to close on seven million.

The BBC enjoyed an almost complete monopoly for its two programmes, The Home Service and The Forces Programme. From Tuesday 6 June 1944, D Day, the corporation introduced a War Report, just after the main evening news. This programme provided listeners with a kaleidoscopic picture, in sound, of the whole, complex field of battle. It was undoubtedly new and exciting, and its night-by-night coverage of the war subsequently proved a huge critical and popular success. Never before had war reporting included the telling details, the miniature narratives, which made human sense of the conflict. It had a troubled relationship with the government that was anxious to ensure that inevitable setbacks on foreign battlefields should not damage public morale at home. The BBC on the other hand, was equally concerned to protect its credibility as a trusted communicator of important information, and was to find itself gradually emerging as a trusted national institution.

Besides providing a blow-by-blow account of the War's progress, the BBC was tasked to make programmes that nurtured public morale on the Home Front. One of its most popular wartime series was It's That Man Again – or, as it was better known, ITMA. By 1944 nearly 40 per cent of the population was listening every week.

The maintenance of morale was not just an issue of reaching the listener at home. In wartime, there were thousands of men and women working in civilian defence bases, such as anti-aircraft batteries. Many millions more were working in factories. They too needed cheering up if the war-effort was to stay on track – and, in particular, the flow of armaments kept up. Consequently, programmes such as Workers' Playtime broadcast uncomplicated live entertainment from factory canteens around the country. By 1942, seven million were tuning-in regularly, many of them from home. In June 1940. Music While You Work provided non-stop music specially designed for those on the production-lines, but listened to by the whole country. Vera Lynn, known as the 'Forces Sweetheart', hosted her own radio programme where she sang and passed on messages from their families to troops serving overseas.

It was through the radio that the public were made aware of the ultimate horror of the War In April 1945, as the allied armies advanced into Germany, they discovered a network of Nazi concentration camps in which the extermination of hundreds of thousands of people had become an industry.

The BBC's senior war correspondent, Richard Dimbleby, was the first broadcaster to enter a camp in the otherwise unremarkable town of Bergen-Belsen. No report from any front resonated for so long or so terribly as his description of what he found. He was quite overcome by what he saw and broke down several times while making his report. He described the scenes of almost unimaginable horror that greeted him - approximately 60,000 prisoners inside, most of them half-starved and seriously ill, and another 13,000 corpses lying around the camp unburied. He said that this day at Belsen was the most horrible of his life. His description of what he saw there was so graphic that the BBC declined to broadcast his despatch for four days, relenting only when he threatened to resign. An edited version was eventually aired, with references to Jews removed.

Unsurprisingly, the nation was horrified. The Rector wrote...

> .....*We have all, naturally and rightly, been horrified by the appalling accounts of atrocities in the German Concentration Camps, and the reaction to this horror is a feeling of complete detestation for the vile perpetrators of such ghastly deeds. In fact, it is almost impossible to realise how a human being can reach such a degraded state that he can calmly and deliberately behave as these people behave. It only goes to show how depraved man can become if he rejects God and the Gospel and the Commandments of Jesus Christ. However, there is a very real danger that we include in our righteous abhorrence, many men and women who, far from being guilty of atrocious crimes against humanity, are themselves the victims of these crimes.*

The German Concentration Camps have been in existence for ten years or more. Their first inmates were not members of other races (sic), but were Germans and German Jews. England, including our own Parish (Flint Hall)[43], gave shelter to the children of these Germans although only comparatively few[44] could be got over to our country. Even now a large percentage of the inhabitants of these camps are German opponents of the Nazi regime. Consequently, to say that the unveiling of the horrors in these camps prove once and for all that all Germans are villains of the worst type, and that therefore, the whole German race should be eliminated is both unjust and ludicrous.

It may well be held by many people that, because he has submitted to the Nazi regime, the German in every walk of life is guilty of the crimes committed by his government. There are obviously large numbers of Germans who now claim to be anti-Nazi but who are only so in name. Many thousands of genuine anti-Nazis, no doubt, have remained quiescent when they might have shown a braver face. But it must be remembered that tens of thousands have spoken openly and have suffered for their courage. In to-day's Times (April 23rd), I read that in the German section at Buchenwald Concentration Camp there are 3,000

---

[43] A house on the Skirmett road.

[44] WW tells us that 'over 2,000 Jewish immigrants from Germany, Poland and other countries found a temporary home at Flint Hall before moving on elsewhere.'

German opponents of Hitler. Yes, and how many more thousands perished in that camp alone.

Secondly, we cannot realise in this country what it is to live in constant fear of an authority which is all powerful, and which is no more benevolent to its own people who may stand in its way than to its enemies outside the national frontiers. Constant fear is a terrible thing and produces terrible results.

So, it is true surely to say that, although we may have the right to judge the ordinary German for his part in the general panorama of horror, yet we cannot condemn all Germans out of hand for these particular crimes. The Nazis have been proved to be detestable by every standard, but it will be unjust by our own standards and unwise for the future of Europe and the World, if one does not think calmly and plan in a Christian way for the future of Germany and its inhabitants. 1945.5

As Bob Dylan was to write some eighteen years later...

The Second World War came to an end
We forgave the Germans, and then we were friends
Though they murdered six million, in the ovens they fried
The Germans now too have God on their side

Another way that the public kept themselves up to date was through the medium of the British Movietone News. This was the only means they had of seeing moving pictures of the War and other events. The newsreel was updated each week and shown before the feature film in all cinemas.

When war was declared on 3rd September 1939, the government ordered all cinemas and places of entertainment to be closed due to fear of bombing. 'What agent of Chancellor Hitler is it who has suggested that we should all cower in darkness and terror 'for the duration'?', asked George Bernard Shaw in a letter to The Times. As Shaw put it, denying entertainment to soldiers and civilians was 'a masterstroke of unimaginative stupidity'. The result was so drab that the nation despaired. Calls were quickly raised to re-open the cinemas and within two weeks the restrictions were lifted.

Going to the cinema was an extremely popular pastime; between 25 and 30 million cinema tickets were sold weekly. Not only did cinemas provide entertainment, but they also enabled folks to escape into the comforts and luxurious surrounding which the cinema provided.

Villagers would get the bus to the original Regal cinema in Henley built on the site of what is now the Waitrose supermarket. It had only been recently opened (1937), designed in a Neo-Georgean style on the exterior and had an Art Deco style interior.[45]

The epic American film *Gone With The Wind* (1940), starring English actress Vivien Leigh, was the smash hit of the war, but British films such as *In Which We Serve* (1942) and *Millions Like Us* (1943) were also highly successful. One film was shot locally, in Turville - *Went the Day Well?* (1942) The film, notable for its unusually frank, for the time, depiction of ruthless violence, reinforced the message that civilians should be vigilant against fifth columnists and that 'careless talk costs lives'. By the time the film was released the threat of invasion had subsided somewhat, but it was still seen as an effective piece of propaganda and its reputation has grown over the years., In the film, people of all classes and backgrounds, with one notable exception, come together to do the decent thing and fight back to defend their homes and one another. The elderly vicar; the lady in the manor house; the chatty, simple-hearted shopkeeper, the poacher and his boy — all of them and more band together to face down a threat that arrives cloaked in benign bonhomie. The County Council allowed the addition of a shop, house, pump, and porch for location filming in May and June 1942 provided they were removed within two months. It provided the first significant role of Thora Hird's career.

The Independent on Sunday commented in 2010, '*It subtly captures an immemorial quality of English rural life—the church, the local gossip, the*

---

[45] The cinema closed without warning in May 1986 and was demolished in December 1993.

sense of community—and that streak of native 'pluck' that people believed would see off Hitler.'

Although newsprint was rationed after 1942, newspapers played a vital role in shaping public opinion and government policy during the War. Lord Hambleden provided daily papers to the reading room in the Working Men's Institute.

Eighty percent of British families read a paper. By 1945, the Daily Express and the Daily Mirror had the largest circulations, between them selling over 7.5 million copies daily. The outstanding Sunday title was the News of the World with a circulation of nearly 8 million. Unheard of numbers today (as is the News of the World!)

Most families in the village either had, or had access to, a copy of Picture Post. It began publishing in 1938, and by December 1943, the magazine was selling 1,950,000 copies a week. Its success was down to its stance on politics, being liberal, anti-fascist, and populist. From its inception, it campaigned against the persecution of Jews in Nazi Germany. Some of its vaguely titillating covers also may have had something to do with its success! Here is the cover of the April 16, 1941 edition.

The War not only changed the way villagers thought but also the way they spoke. Through the radio, newspapers, the cinema and the presence of American servicemen, many new words, and new interpretations of old words, left their mark on the nation's vocabulary. The heightened conditions of warfare provide a boost to the human propensity to use jargon, slang and bad language. In warfare, the new and unfamiliar require fresh terminology.

Among the new words that the 1939-45 war gave English are some borrowed from our enemies: kamikaze, flak, and ersatz. The unique enormity of German wartime atrocities brought a new word into the language – genocide. Radar is a US coinage from 1940, taken from the initial letters of 'radio detection and ranging'. RDF – the British equivalent initialism – was quickly replaced by the catchier American acronym.

The Royal Air Force (whose aircrew suffered the highest death rates of all British service personnel) was a rich source of new words: bandits (hostile aircraft), stooging (flying aimlessly), get weaving (start briskly), going for a burton (being killed), shaky dos, (close shaves), prangs

"Hey, half a minute, half a minute! 'Shooting a line', 'Putting up a black', 'Going for a burton', 'Taking a dim view' -- what kind of language is that?"

(crashes) and tail-end Charlies (rear gunners). All became familiar to a villager following the pilots' exploits.

Perhaps the most enduring slogan of the wartime vocabulary is the phrase designed by the Government in 1939 to be used as a motivational poster. It was intended to raise morale and to reflect British resilience: Keep Calm and Carry On.

****

As we've seen Hambleden loved to dance. Dancing played a huge part in keeping up morale during the War. The 1940s dance styles were all centred around swing dance, made popular by young Americans (of which there were thousands in the Henley area) who adopted the movements to fit with the emerging sounds of rock 'n roll. Bandleaders Artie Shaw, Benny Goodman and Glen Miller from America and Brits Victor Silvestor, Harry Roy and Joe Loss were all very popular.

The Home Guard organised at least one event. Not to be outdone…..

> … *The Football Club has organised two Dances and one Whist Drive and Dance which together realized the splendid sum of £10/7/10. This amount is earmarked for the lads of the village who are serving with the Forces. We are very grateful indeed to the lads of the Football Club who worked like Trojans.* 1941.1

As part of the victory celebrations…….

> *some enthusiastic folk danced until nearly 4 in the morning!*
> 1945.6

Chapter 8

Fawley Court[46]

Seeing servicemen and women in and around the village was common. In particular, the sight of young women who were part of the First Aid Nursing Yeomanry (FANY) would have been familiar. Although not part of the regular army, they were distinguished by their quasi-military outfits – a khaki women's officers' uniform with a wide leather belt and FANY buttons, lapel and hat badges. They wore the chinstrap of their caps over the crown.

But they were not off-duty nurses – they were members of a secret wireless training centre at Fawley Court, perhaps seeking a decent meal at the pub, or simply doing a bit of shopping.

Fawley Court is a riverside mansion, which although closer to Henley than Hambleden, is within the Hambleden Parish boundaries. The entrance seems innocuous enough, apart from some rather splendid gates – a screen

---

[46] Much of this section is based on research conducted by the Rev Sue Morton, to whom I am most grateful.

of trees makes it difficult to see what lies beyond. It was only the presence of sentries at these gates during the War that hinted that here was something official going on behind them.

Early in the War, London museums had to evacuate their contents to prevent them from being destroyed by bombs. The Natural History Museum evacuated its collections to various country houses outside London[47]. One such house was Fawley Court. Its owner, Major Mackenzie, received over 300 cabinets from the entomology department, together with their associated staff. Unsurprisingly, he was less than pleased about this, and arguments between Mackenzie and the museum deteriorated into questions of how to split the heating bill. But problems relating to the storage of dead bugs on pins soon faded into the background. Worse was yet to come, for in 1940, Fawley Court was requisitioned for use by the Special Operations Executive (SOE).

Damage to the NHM's Shell Gallery, c. 1940.

SOE was a vital part of the Resistance as disrupters of the Germans' plans, be it by destroying telephone lines, by blowing up railways or by collecting

---

[47] Thanks to these evacuations, most of the NHM's collection survived the war intact. Had it remained in London, many objects would have been destroyed. Between September 1940 and April 1941, the Natural History Museum was hit by oil and incendiary bombs in several air raids.

information about troop movements and relaying it to London on concealed radios designed to look like suitcases. The new force had an influential supporter in Prime Minister Winston Churchill, who famously ordered them to 'set Europe ablaze!'

Membership of SOE was by invitation only and the agents were a vital cog in supporting the Allies pre and post D-Day. There was a rank structure but gender equality was paramount with all agents undergoing the same training and selection, which was based entirely on ability. Those who accepted their role were under no illusion of the type of warfare that they would be involved in.

Fawley Court was used as a wireless training centre for those in the SOE who had volunteered to be agents working in Europe behind enemy lines, and for those at home who would keep wireless contact with them. Its existence was so secret that not even the army high command knew about it. Fawley's importance as an SOE base has long been overlooked: although its work is no longer a secret[48], even today not many people know about its existence. It was our own little Bletchley Park.

SOE realised that hundreds, if not thousands, of wireless operators would be required over the course of the war, so they set about recruiting them. After an interview, girls[49]'of good background, quiet tongues and quick

---

[48] Not so secret perhaps. One story, perhaps apocryphal, tells of a recruit who missed his train and hailed a taxi in London. He asked the driver if he knew Fawley Court, near Henley-on-Thames. The driver replied "Sure…..That's where they train all the spies"!! (Bob McFarlane – Funeral Eulogy by Andre Saunders, February 16, 2017)

[49] Some men were also trained.

brains ', who perhaps were good at knitting or could play the piano, found themselves on an induction course at Overthorpe Manor, near Banbury. There they were asked to sign the Official Secrets Act. None of them knew what they were being recruited for; not even their parents knew what they were doing. They were told that their daughters were being trained as drivers.

After Overthorpe, the girls were sent to Special Training School (STS) 52d, Fawley Court in batches of up to 150 at a time. Many of the women at Fawley Court were enlisted into the First Aid Nursing Yeomanry (FANY) to disguise their secret work. FANY had been formed in 1907 as a first aid link between the field hospitals and the front lines during the Great War, and was given the 'yeomanry' suffix as its members were originally mounted on horseback. By 1939 there was no need for horses, and FANY women were trained in one of four fields: motor transport (In which Princess Elizabeth had been a member), wireless telegraphy, codes or general. The telegraphy unit morphed into the SOE.

When they were founded, the FANY was unashamedly elitist. It was a Yeomanry, an organisation for the daughters of the land-owning classes who could ride horses. To a great extent it had preserved that ethos up to the beginning of World War II. Many of the young women members had been 'debs', had been presented at court and 'done the season'; some even had titles. Their education had concentrated on subjects like deportment and the correct way to address a viscount[50]. And, presciently as it would turn out,

---

[50] Useful if they ever were to bump into Lord Hambleden!

French. To some of the women, Henley would have been familiar, having attended regattas before the War.

The recruitment drive required the influx of a large number of girls from very different backgrounds; there were no allowances made for class at Fawley Court. As one trainee, Jane Buckland, remembered, they all had to muck in, army style....

> ....*We were all required to do our share of square-bashing, marching and washing up. We were real dogsbodies, absolutely; we were lower than low. All these aristocratic girls were now doing square bashing and washing. We all were treated quite toughly.*

Living conditions at Fawley Court left a lot to be desired. Male agents had to  put up with bunks made of plywood with straw mattresses, and little more than a cold-water pipe in the stable yard for a shower. The girls slept in spartan attics in the house which were freezing cold in winter and claustrophobic in summer. Telegraphy training took place in a complex of huts in the grounds. By the end of the War over 3,000 FANYs had served with SOE - as trainers, coders, signallers, forgers, dispatchers, and, most famously, as agents. Of the 50 women sent by SOE into France 39 were members of the FANY. Of these 39 women, 12 were murdered by the Nazis and one member was killed in action.

The training course at Fawley Court lasted for three to four months. The

course was technically challenging. Apart from learning to send and receive morse code accurately at a sufficient speed, over twenty words per minute, recruits needed to understand radio wave propagation and the use of cyphers. They needed to recognise the 'fist' of the agent they would be working with, as morse code is as individual to the operator as handwriting. Every radio operator had a different style of tapping out morse code, and no two hands are the same.

Messages were in code and sent in groups of five letters which did not make words, so if one letter was missed it was impossible to guess what it should have been, and they were often sent in haste and in poor atmospheric conditions. It was intensive and demanding work.

Potential agents had to learn how to repair their wireless in the field. They also needed to prove their competence in the use of various security measures intended to make it difficult for German direction finders pin-pointing the safe houses agents were using whilst in contact with their handlers. Those that volunteered to operate behind enemy lines were the only women permitted a combat role during the Second World War. Most worked in France, where it was felt women could move around much more freely, because, since over 1.6 million French men had been deported by the Germans into forced labour, male resistance fighters were dangerously conspicuous. The FANY agent had to have perfect knowledge of France, very good (though not necessarily perfect) French, and few family ties.

When they reached the required speeds in morse they were posted to Grendon Underwood, off the A41 between Aylesbury and Bicester.

Each FANY field agent had his/her own team of handlers that were on duty 24 hours a day. The handlers gave each agent a small token of humanity before their departure into the field, such as a compact, lipstick or perfume – and, of course, their deadly cyanide pill.

Intensive work it may have been, but there were plenty of distractions during the FANYs' time off. "There was never a dull evening," one recruit recalled. "You were either in the recreation hut with dancing, music, darts . . . or we played tennis.' What she failed to mention was the presence of American officers stationed at Phyllis Court, only a few hundred yards away, connected, conveniently, by an avenue of trees!

> *(In August 1941, the Air Ministry requisitioned Phyllis Court in Henley. Ladies from the Photographic Reconnaissance Unit moved in and spent nine months meticulously scanning aerial photographs of enemy-occupied territory. They were replaced in the summer of 1942 by a small group of American soldiers.*
>
> *Phyllis Court returned to a WAAF (Women's Auxiliary Air Force) hostel in the latter half of 1943. One resident, WAAF Section Officer Jean Fotheringham of Sussex, was married to an*

American officer, Lieutenant L Earl Hollinger at St Mary the Virgin, Hambleden on 15 September 1944.)[51]

Christmas 1943 was a memorable one at the house. The agents and their wireless operators all met up before the launch of Operation Jedburgh[52]. The American officers, with their access to luxuries such as soap, deodorant and cigarettes were very popular with the young wireless operators, much to the chagrin of the English. A New Year's Eve party was held in the Saloon, with music provided by a piano there. Some French agents who had come to train with them allegedly discovered a cellar full of Chateau Haut-Beron[53] that had been laid down by the Mackenzies during 1870-1 and had been forgotten about.[54] Perhaps a few bottles of the Haut-Beron were cracked! Who said that sex was invented in 1963?!

The huts were only intended to be temporary structures, and, after the War, they fell into disrepair. They have now been demolished without trace. However, parts of their wooden exteriors and floorboards were donated towards the restoration of Huts 3 and 6 at Bletchley Park, to keep them true to their wartime origins.

_____

[51] The Times 20 September 1944

[52] Operation Jedburgh was a clandestine operation during World War II in which three-man teams of operatives of the British Special Operations Executive (SOE), the U.S. Office of Strategic Services (OSS), the Free French Bureau central de renseignements et d'action ("Central Bureau of Intelligence and Operations") and the Dutch and Belgian armies in exile were dropped by parachute into occupied France, the Netherlands and Belgium.

[53] If you are lucky enough to track down a bottle of the 1870 Haut-Beron, please contact me!

[54] Information supplied by Mrs Aida Dellal, the owner of Fawley Court.

Fawley Court 2003. Huts clearly visible.

Fawley Court 2017. Huts in poor repair

Fawley Court 2018. Huts demolished

Chapter 9

The National Trust

It had been rumoured for some time that Lord Hambleden was in discussions with the National Trust over the future guardianship of the Estate. In 1944, he entered into a restrictive covenant with the Trust covering over 4,500 acres of the Estate to safeguard the Hambleden Valley from injurious development,[55] which would make building development in the covenanted area well-nigh impossible. It still applies to this day, much to the chagrin of many villagers. This is why the built form of the village looks very much as it did in 1944, and why the village has now become a centre for day trippers, cyclists and walkers. It was not so in 1944.

As you would expect the Rector shared his views on the arrangement with his parishioners....

> *Readers of the Parish Magazine who are living away from home may be interested to hear of an arrangement which Lord Hambleden has made with the National Trust whereby the beauties of Hambleden Village and of the Greenlands Estate as a whole will be safeguarded in the future.*
>
> *The Estate has not been handed over to the National Trust, nor will the owner's relations with his tenants be affected in any way.*

---

[55] Although it is known as the Greenlands covenant, Lord Hambleden deliberately excluded Greenlands House and its grounds because he wanted it to become a training college.

He has, however, covenanted with the Trust that the property, apart from certain areas which have been omitted from the scheme for development purposes, will remain in its present state as agricultural land. He will however be able to build agricultural cottages and farm buildings or other such buildings as may he needed for various purposes on the land covered by the covenant, thus ensuring that it will be used to the best possible purpose.

The National Trust have become owners of four 'view-points' (?) which will be open to the public, and each of which offers a panorama of the Greenlands Estate. As heretofore, the public, and in particular the people of Hambleden, are encouraged to use any of the many walks and rides through the woods, so long as dogs are kept within bounds.

We may hope that through this scheme the country which we all love so well will appear as lovely to our children and grandchildren as it does to us in 1944   1944.8

Chapter 10

War and the Church

Over all this hive of activity presided the Church, and in particular Rector Wilfred Watts. It seems to me that Hambleden was particularly fortunate in having Rector Watts as its spiritual leader. He was a man of some energy and sensitivity. Notwithstanding Lord Hambleden, it was to him that the villagers looked for guidance and it was he that kept the village going during the darkest days of the War. His role was appreciated by Lord Hambleden in a letter to the Times[57]....

> ....It is of the greatest importance that the duties of the Church at home should be emphasized at this time. Quite rightly much has been heard of the activities of the Chaplains to the Forces, and their work should be appreciated to the full. At the same time, no one can doubt the equal importance of the work of the Church at home. In town and country parishes, and particularly in those areas to which children have been evacuated, the work of the parish priest is of the greatest importance to the future of our race (sic).
>
> It will be clear to them that by carrying out the quiet and often humdrum work of a parish they are not only doing their duty to their parishioners, who need more than the usual care in war-

---

[57] 7 December 1939

> time, but also are laying the foundation of an active Christianity for the England of the future.

The Rector was immensely respected and influential. The Parish Magazines reflect his struggle to persuade the villagers to attend church on Sundays, and it is fair to say that most seemed to obey his ministrations.

However, as a committed pacifist, he must have found the position of the Church of England difficult – to reconcile his pacifism and the teachings of Jesus Christ with the position of the established Church, which was to support the state's position in going to War. One may imagine that he would pray that Hitler would have some sort of change of heart in a damascene moment. You will see from his occasional reflections in the Parish Magazine that The Rector struggled to square the circle of 'Love thine enemy' with wartime slaughter, especially of civilians. His notes on the surrender of Japan in August 1945, included as an Appendix, are particularly moving.

A poem from the Great War that perhaps would have resonated with Rector Watts:

> *God heard the embattled nations sing and shout*
>
> *"Gott strafe England!" and "God save the King!"*
>
> *God this, God that, and God the other thing—*
>
> *"Good God!" said God, "I've got my work cut out."* [58]

---

[58] JC Squire 1916

As well as his spiritual duties, the Rector attempted, through the Parish Magazines, to put the War into some sort of context for his parishioners. It was to a packed church[59] that he described movingly the announcement of the outbreak of war in 1939. Thereafter, his notes in the Parish Magazine reflect his varying moods as the War progressed.

The British Expeditionary Force, which grew to 390,000 men over the winter of 1939–40, deployed alongside the troops of its allies in France and Belgium. The force was dug in along the borders facing their opponents, but there was no fighting - a period of anticipation that became known as the Phoney War......

> .....The War has been with us for eight months and we are still waiting for the blow to fall on this country. The air raids which we all expected in September have not yet taken place. Battles have not shattered the opposing armies on the Western front. The people of England have not suffered privations, nor have they had to face the real horrors of modern warfare - and so we are driven back on ourselves and on our power to deal with the strange situation which faces us today.   1940.5

The rector spoke too soon. The Phoney War became a real war on 9 May 1940 when the German armed forces mobilised. Their attack punched through the defending French forces and proceeded to race across northern France, causing confusion and disarray. With no strategic Allied reserve or

---

[59] Hambleden Parish Magazine November 2023.

counterattack of any strength to stop them, just a week later German advance forces reached the English Channel near Abbeville, at the mouth of the river Somme. By the last week of May 1940, most of the BEF together with a large French contingent and some Belgian soldiers were trapped by the German army in a restricted area around the small French port of Dunkerque. Their evacuation by sea was imperative, but assessments of success were gloomy.

We all know what happened next. On the evening of 26 May an amphibious rescue was set in motion. Over the next nine days, the Royal Navy's fighting ships, merchant transport vessels and small civilian boats of all kinds plied the dangerous waters to and from Dunkerque under frequent and intense German attacks from land, sea and air. The operation came to a close in the early hours of 4 June. By the end of the day, 338,226 British and Allied troops had been rescued and landed in England.

It was a dark time in the history of Europe. With the British army in disarray, an imminent invasion by German troops was expected. Preparations to protect the civilian population had already been made in the years leading up to 1939, and naturally, these efforts were stepped up after the Dunkerque evacuation. Air raid shelters were constructed in many gardens in Hambleden, gas masks were issued to everyone and arrangements were made for the evacuation of children from major cities. By the end of 1940, 40 evacuee children were attending Hambleden school.

Jim Tilbury remembers...

> .....When the siren went in Henley, my mother and I would sleep under the dining room table. My father was out on ARP patrol, making sure that the village was 'blacked out'. Later we built an Anderson shelter in our garden. The government supplied pre-formed sheets of corrugated iron.

In September of 1940, after Churchill had offered blood, toil, tears and sweat, and after he had roused the nation with his peroration to fight in the fields, in the streets and in the hills, the Parish Magazine included the following statement from the Archbishop of Canterbury...

> .....the anxieties and responsibilities of the nation and Empire have been greatly increased. The defection (sic)[60] by the Government of France has left us alone among the nations of Western Europe to defend the cause of justice and freedom against unscrupulous and ruthless aggression. The invasion of our own land by the enemy is threatened, and may at any time be attempted.[61]
>
> 1940.9

Seven months later the Rector let his parishioners be in no doubt that the threat was still apparent....

---

[60] The Germans eventually broke through the French line, and succeeded in taking Paris on 14 June. On 22 June the French signed an armistice, surrendering to the Germans.

[61] By October 1940, almost everyone expected an invasion. (WW)

> *...It is generally anticipated that during the next few months our country will be more severely tried than at any other time during this War, and that the future of civilisation will depend largely upon how we face up to these trials both nationally and individually.* 1941.4

A year later things had not got any better. We can detect the mood of despondency in the Rector's words as he tried to rally his flock to the cause....

> *....The great anxieties of these early days of 1942, the feelings of depression and frustration from which we all suffer in our daily lives, have affected us all of late. The end of the War and the beginning of a saner and truer life seem further away than ever, and we are forced to steel ourselves to face an immediate future which is grim in the extreme. We cannot doubt that it is time for us to take stock; to set our teeth with an even grimmer determination and, above all, to search our hearts for the weaker places which must be made strong enough to withstand the ordeals to come.*

> *On all sides we hear calls for an even greater national effort - for a solid will to face up to all disasters in order to win through to final victory - but very rarely do we hear of the ways and means to make ourselves strong and fit to endure, to conquer! To conquer - but to conquer whom or what enemy?*

> *To be in a position to win this War is not enough. To be strong enough to overcome our enemies in the field spells merely temporary and illusory victory in itself. We have much further to go than this if we count ourselves to be true Christians and true Patriots. The very urgency of the times; the changes from day to day and the general atmosphere of anxiety and instability all militate against clear and steady thinking. But if we pause for a moment and force ourselves to face the facts, we must know that our failings and our lack of understanding can be cured only by a complete surrender to God and to His will.*   1942.3

Six months on, he bemoaned that prayer seemed to have scant effect....

> *....His Majesty the King has appealed to the nation to observe September 3rd as a Day of Prayer. Since that tragic day three years ago when War broke out we have had a number of days of prayer. These have had varying success, but do not, in fact, seem to have made much lasting impression on the nation as a whole.*   1942.9

A month later he noted that winter....

> *.....would soon be upon us, so don't forget to bring your greatcoats and rugs and your hot water bottles to church for we cannot promise that the church will be as warm as in past years.*
>   1942.10

After several setbacks in the Western Desert, the allies finally overcame the enemy at El Alamein in November 1942. Churchill felt he could declare *'Now this is not the end. It is not even the beginning of the end. But it is, perhaps,* the end of the beginning',[62] the Bishop of Oxford was able to take a more positive line in his letter to his parishioners.....

> As I look back over the year 1942 I see three great series of events which should give to us in this diocese confidence and great hope for the future.
>
> In the terrible yet epoch-making history of the War, the first eight months of the year will be set down as among the worst which our country has ever experienced. The tragedies of the Far East, the disasters in North Africa, the danger of the great U-boat attacks, the vast Russian setbacks - here, if ever, were grounds for the gravest anxiety.
>
> But with the autumn the whole aspect of the War began to change, and at the moment at which I write we are full of hope although over and over again we are warned by those best qualified to judge that we have much tribulation yet to endure.
>
> We are told that the final victory is not yet even in sight and efforts greater than any hitherto are now demanded of us.
>
> 1943.2

Six months later the worst seemed to be over. The War had been in progress nearly four years, and people in the parish (though I daresay, not in London

---

[62] Mansion House speech, 10 November 1942.

and other cities) had adjusted their lifestyles to it. The Bishop thought it fit to warn his diocese against boredom.....

> ......Boredom is something of which we have all had vivid experience. There has been a good deal of it even in this War. The first six months, when things marched so slowly that outside observers spoke of the War as 'phoney' - the period when, after intense activity, amazing victory, or humiliating defeat, a curtain had fallen upon events, whilst the next phase of each different campaign was maturing. Since then, eager expectation or vivid anxiety have gradually faded away, to be succeeded by a vague wondering as to what will happen next, and so to mere boredom with the drab routine of everyday life. This state of boredom is dangerous. It means a relaxation of tension and activity, a loss of spiritual vitality, a growth of inertia. It is in moments such as these that all kinds of temptations present themselves with deadly effect. 1943.8

By the end of 1943, after victories at EL Alamein, Stalingrad and Kursk, victory and peace seemed possible, but the Rector found he could not rejoice wholeheartedly. His words give a hint of what was to come in the General Election of 1945......

> ....Of course, we can have the type of peace which reigned in Europe before this War, but who wants this kind of peace - the peace before a mighty storm ? The peace without goodwill ? The peace which was content to allow millions to be unemployed without decent homes and with hardly the bare necessities of

life, and which calmly looked on whilst nations were subjugated and tens of millions of people enslaved.

And if this is the only kind of peace we are going to know after the War, all the suffering caused by this bestial War will have been in vain. Men will have given their lives for nothing. Women and children in our own country and on the continent in their tens of thousands will have been slaughtered only to pave the way for an even greater slaughter in years to come. For, make no mistake, peace without goodwill can never rise above being an armistice - and an armistice is only another term for a short truce - until one side or the other is ready to commence hostilities again. What we want is goodwill between nation and nation and between peoples within every nation - between class and class and employer and employed - the spirit of give and take.

Let us not then think that peace is the only thing that matters and that everything in the garden is bound to be lovely when the War is over. It will only be after hostilities have ceased that the greatest test will come. 1943.12

In March 1944, there was a mass escape from the POW camp Stalag Luft 111, since immortalised in the film '*The Great Escape*'. Of the 76 escapees, 73 were recaptured. Of these, 50 were executed. The British government learned of the deaths from a routine visit to the camp by Swiss authorities as the protecting power in May. The Foreign Secretary, Anthony Eden, announced the news to the House of Commons on 19 May 1944.

The nation was quite shocked. The Rector wrote.....

> ....The tragedy of Stalag Luft 111 has caused the deepest distress and concern. Every prisoner who plans to escape (and who would not if the opportunity arose) knows that he runs the risk of being killed or wounded, but it is a significant fact, as the Times pointed out, that whereas forty-seven prisoners were killed outright and fifteen recaptured, not one is reported to have been wounded. The whole Country is waiting for fuller information with profound anxiety.   1944.6

In September 1944, the Rector continued where he had left off in December 1943...

> ....Victory is certainly in the air and may be ours at any moment now - at least as far as the War in Europe is concerned. Peace before Christmas is not merely what we hope and pray for but what we even expect! But peace will have its problems and difficulties as any thinking person must surely realise and as many papers now are warning us. No peace which does not seek to promote the welfare of all nations will stand the test of time. A peace of vengeance or a selfish peace will be no peace at all, but only an armistice leading up to an even more horrible War. War is caused not by one man or by one nation but by the greed and selfishness of man as a whole. One nation may be responsible for it more than another and be the immediate cause of it - starting the ball rolling - but social unrest, bad economic conditions, unemployment on a large scale and such

> *evils, caused by individual and national greed, are the root causes of War.*
>
> *1944.9*

One cannot help feeling that the Rector was pushing against the grain. Even though the United Nations came into being on October 24, 1945, it was only some nineteen weeks later that Churchill introduced the chilling phrase 'iron curtain' to the lexicon. Since then, barely a year has gone by when British forces have not been in action somewhere on the globe. I hope the Rector didn't die a sadly disillusioned man.

Chapter 11

Victory

By the end of October 1944, the end of the War was in sight. The Archbishop of Canterbury was quite prescriptive in what form church celebrations should take...

> ....It may be that the end of the European fighting will come upon us suddenly. I hope that arrangements will be made in every church to hold a solemn service of thanksgiving and rededication at the earliest possible convenient moment after any such news is received. I should like a time to be chosen and notice to be given in advance that on any day on which the announcement of the end of the European fighting is made, if it be before 6 p.m. there will be a service in the church that evening at a time of which everybody is aware in advance. In each parish the time should be fixed to suit the convenience of the people, but it should, if possible, be announced early; the sooner the better, so that everyone may know that on that day if they come together they will find a congregation united in praise, thanksgiving and dedication. I suggest that in all cases the Te Deum should be sung at this service. 1944.10

Before they were stood down on 31 December 1944, The Home Guard geared themselves up for welcome home festivities...

> ....A Committee has been chosen by No. 6 Platoon (Hambleden) 4 Bucks Bn. Home Guard and Civil Defence Services to collect and administer a fund that will enable us to welcome home those men and women who have served in H.M. Forces, during the present War. The fund will operate within the boundaries defined by the area under the supervision of the Police Station at Mill End, and in the main, will embrace the villages of Fawley, Hambleden (with Pheasants Hill and Colstrope), and Medmenham (with Bockmer). With a substantial fund in hand, it is proposed that each Service man or woman from the above area will on his or her return receive a tribute. Due consideration will be given to those who are absent for any length of time after an European peace. There are some, too, who can never return and their kinsfolk will not to forgotten. In addition to these personal tributes, it is hoped that there will be a substantial balance available to help those ex-service people who for reasons beyond their control find themselves in temporary need of financial aid. 1944.11

ER's recollection, however, is somewhat different....

> ..... I didn't think anything special was done for returning soldiers. They just had to get on with it. They were treated awfully as far as I was concerned. No support.

So, unlike the armistice of 1918, when the guns stopped firing and the soldiers burst out of their trenches at precisely 11 o'clock on the 11th November 1918, in 1945 the war in Germany petered out while politicians argued about when the celebrations might begin. On May 1st the BBC interrupted regular programmes to announce that Hitler was dead. No further comment followed. Later that day they announced that Berlin had fallen. On May 3rd Hamburg surrendered. On May 4th General Montgomery received the surrender of all German forces in Denmark, Netherlands and NW Germany at Luneburg Heath. The unconditional surrender of the German Third Reich wasn't signed until the early morning hours of Monday, May 7, 1945, at Supreme Headquarters, Allied Expeditionary Force at Reims. That should have been VE Day, but the Russians objected; they insisted on a formal ceremony in Berlin.

The sense of anticipation in the village was palpable. By Monday morning, 7th of May, there was still no definite news. The War was over, it seemed, but peace had not yet begun. Villagers were getting restless and impatient for an announcement. Were they expected to keep on going to work? When would they be allowed to celebrate after almost six years of sacrifice and deprivation? Like the phoney war, this was the phoney peace. Everyone seemed unsettled, half excited and half exhausted, as if torn between joy that the war was over and, at last, the freedom to admit what an ordeal it had been. A strange atmosphere of weary depression hung over the village.

The mood was broken when, at 3pm on Tuesday, May 8th, Churchill broadcast to the country that the German War was at an end. Everyone sat and listened to the Prime Minister's address on the radio in the same sort of respectful silence they might observe for the King or for Rector Watts' weekly sermon. And, indeed, his talk was rather like a sermon.

He announced that hostilities would end officially at one minute after midnight tonight. He reminded everyone that some of the Germans were still fighting the Russian troops, but said that this should not prevent us from celebrating today and tomorrow as victory in Europe days. Today, perhaps, he droned on, we will think mostly of ourselves. Tomorrow we shall pay a particular tribute to our Russian comrades, whose prowess in the field has been one of the grand contributions to the general victory. The German war, the Prime Minister continued, is therefore at an end. We may allow ourselves a brief period of rejoicing, but let us not forget for a moment the toil and efforts that lie ahead. Japan, with all her treachery and greed, remained unsubdued.

At last!

Blackout blankets were removed from windows. Frocks and nylons that had been put aside for just such a day were dug out from drawers and wardrobes. On May 7 the BBC had announced that red, white and blue bunting was off the ration. War weariness was forgotten! Attics were raided, and the village was festooned when celebrations began on May 8th.

The village was ready to party!

> *.....To gain an extra hour of daylight for the celebrations, Lord Hambleden had the forestry clear a gap in the woods ('sunset strip'). Lord H had all the estate workers pile up the cut wood until there was a pile some 20ft high. With all the cut wood, they lit a massive great bonfire on top of the hill, and there was a party in the village.*

> *Similar on VJ night[63], another fire but someone set fire to it the night before!*
>
> *JT*

The day began with an intense thunderstorm, but was followed by sunshine and warmth. Victory weather! The rector takes up the story...

> *.....The day started - at least as far as some of us were concerned - with the greatest of all Thanksgiving Services - the Eucharist - and throughout the whole morning people wandered into the church to give thanks. But our official thanksgiving did not commence until after the Prime Minister's speech on the wireless at 3 p.m., when he publicly announced that the War had ended in Europe. Then for a whole hour our church bells[64] rang out their praises to Almighty God for the blessings of Victory and peace. At 6 p.m. the bells pealed out again for another hour, and by 7 p.m. the hour fixed for the Thanksgiving Service, in spite of about a hundred extra chairs, the church was packed to overflowing with worshippers. The Service only lasted about half an hour but I think it will ever remain in the memory of all who attended it. The hymns we sung were "Praise my soul the King of Heaven"; an Easter hymn "The Strife is O'er"; a hymn for conversion of the whole world "Let there be Light" (A & M 360), and "For all the Saints" when we remembered the fallen in*

---

[63] 15 August 1945

[64] During the War, no church bells were permitted to be rung except on the occasion of an invasion. (Wilfred Watts : A Country Pason)

battle, especially those of this parish. During this hymn a collection was taken for "The Million Pound Fund for Christian reconstruction in liberated Europe" which amounted to £264. At the end of the Service, we all sang the Te Deum with the choir facing the Altar, and then followed the blessing,

After the Service most of us went back to supper[65] and listened to the King's speech on the radio at 9pm, and then we went down to the Parish Room where a dance was being held for the Welcome Home[66] Fund. Judging by the crowd I doubt if very much dancing was done, at any rate not at this early hour! At 10 p.m. we all went into the Dene[67] to gather and sing round a really vast bonfire, and while this was going on dozens of fireworks were let off. In the distance we could again hear the bells of our church ringing out their victory peal. The bell ringers worked very hard on this day and we are all most grateful to them. About 11 p.m. many of us went back to the Parish Room and I understand that some enthusiastic folk danced[68] until nearly 4 in the morning!

_____

[65] Or to the pub!

[66] The Fund finally raised £1,500 (over £100,000 today!)

[67] A public recreation area behind the Stag and Huntsman.

[68] Perhaps they practiced the latest American craze of jitterbugging.

At 8am. and 10,30am. the next day, there were celebrations of Holy Communion and at 12 noon a short Thanksgiving Service; at 6.30 we said Evensong.

So ended our two days holiday. 1945.6

So, the War spluttered to a finish. There was nothing neat and tidy about its end nor about the beginning of peace. At the end of the War, there were approximately five million service members in the British Armed Forces, including Charles Gray and butcher Arthur Wheeler. The demobilisation and reassimilation of this vast force back into civilian life was one of the first and greatest challenges facing the postwar British government. For most people the summer of 1945 was a tangle of loose ends, a time of difficult reunions and broken relationships. War widows, of course, celebrated with mixed feelings. Many ex-POWs and demobbed servicemen and women were scarred, some permanently so. Post traumatic stress disorder was not fully understood in 1945. And, of course, the War in the Far East would continue until August 14 when Japan surrendered.

Chapter 12

Afterwards

In the General Election of 1945, the Rector got his wish. The country voted for a change and the Conservative Party was defeated by a landslide. The Labour Party took office, promising social reform. In the Wycombe constituency, a Conservative majority of 16,000 was overturned.

Appendix 1 : Kelly's Directory 1939

HAMBLEDEN.

PRIVATE RESIDENTS.

(For T N's see general list of Private Residents at end of book.)

Beauchamp Douglas C. Varnells
Beever William Frederick Holt J.P. Yewden
Bulteel Mrs., Yewden manor
Claxton Rev. Edward Arthur, The Manse, Pheasants hill
Cripps Hon. Alfred Henry Seddon J.P. Parmoor
Daniel Ernest Edward, Mill house, Mill end
Droughton V. The Wooleys
Elliott Jn. Edwin M.B. Spenithorne
Foster Mrs. Hambleden place
Gask Col. George Ernest C.M.G., D.S.O., F.R.C.S. Hatchmans
George Mrs. Fayland
Gerhardt Misses, North house
Grenfell Miss Maud J.P. Bacres
Hambleden Viscount, Greenlands; & 31 Belgrave square S W 1 & Carlton & Travellers' clubs, London
Howson Mrs. The Hyde
Luard Mrs. B. C. The Cottage
Parmoor Lord P.C., K.C.V.O., J.P. Parmoor
Stainton Mrs. Eleanor Margaret, Manor house
Stobart Edward, Pheasants Coombe
Watts Rev. Wilfred Edwd. M.A. (rector), The Rectory
Wilson Andrew Stewart M.B. Little Colstrope

COMMERCIAL.

Marked thus ° farm 150 acres or over.
°Austin Alfd. Jas. farmer, Pheasants Hill farm
Barksfield Bros. grocers. T N 9
Barnett C. & Sons (James Donaldson & Sons (Oxon.) Ltd. proprs.), millers (water), Hambleden mills. T N 16
°Bowden Jn. farmer, Mill End farm. T N 20
Brown Wm. Hy. gamekeeper to Viscount Hambleden, Dairy la. Greenlands (letters direct from Henley-on-Thames)
Cook Adeline (Miss) S.C.N. district nurse. T N 15
Courtney Alfd. builders' mer
Elliott Jn. Edwin M.B., M.R.C.S., D.R.C.O.G. physcn. & obstetrician (firm. Elliott. Elliott & Gillett), Spenithorne. T N 5
°Emmett Chas. Edwd. farmer, Rockwell End. T N 5
Gibson —. farmer, Rotten Row farm
Hambleden Museum (F. M. Underhill, hon. curator)
Harris Edward John, saddler
Heath Harold P. schoolmaster & clerk to Parish Council. T N 26
Homes of Rest
Keene Alfd. D. farmer, Colstrope. T N 21
Keene Arth. farmer, Rockwell End
°Keene Percvl. farmer, The Roost
°King Geo. Edmnd. farmer, Flint Hall farm. T N 37
Lee William (Butchers) Ltd. T N 41
°Manuel Wltr. farm bailiff to Viscount Hambleden, Yewden farm & Bakers farm. T N 17
Moffat Jn. gardener to Viscount Hambleden, Gardens, Greenlands. T N 19
Plumridge F. laundry, Pheasants Hill
Pheasant P.H. (Wm. Roberts), Pheasants
Sherwin Geo. land steward to Lord Parmoor P.C., K.C.V.O., J.P. Bagmoor
Simmons Lewis, farmer, Luxters farm (letters through Southend, Henley-on-Thames)
Simmons Raymond Harper, farmer, The Beeches, Pheasants. T N 53
Stag & Huntsman P.H. (Geo. Blankstone Gloyne). T N 27
Stag Stores (Sydney Baker, proprietor), high-class grocers; off licence. Pheasants hill. T N 28
Tilbury Sidney, blacksmith, oxyacetylene welder, ornamental ironworker & wheelwright
°Walker Rt. farmer, Hutton's farm
Webb Arth. Thos. shopkpr. & post office
Wiltshire Herbt. Jas. farmer, Little Parmoor farm
Wise H. W. painter

Appendix 2 : Hambleden Village Centre 1945

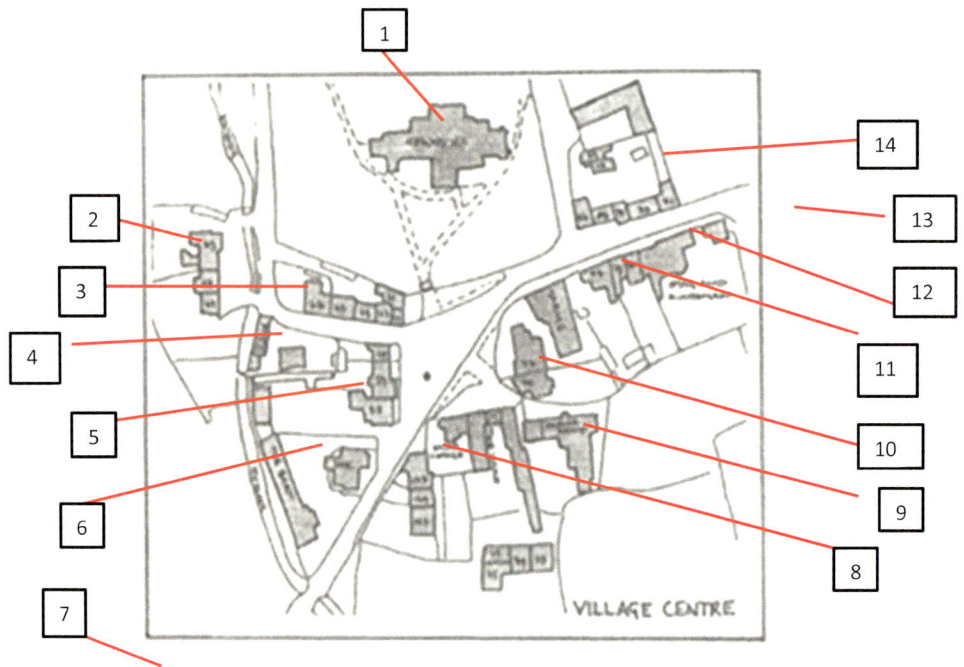

1. Church
2. Bakery/Stores (Saxby)
3. The Forge (home of the Tilburys)
4. Blacksmith (Sid Tilbury)
5. Village Post Office/Stores/Telephone Exchange/Stores (Arthur Webb)
6. Men's Institute
7. The school (not on map)
8. Builders Merchant (Alf Courtney)
9. Village Hall/ Parish Rooms/ old school
10. Saddler / Harness maker (Ted Harris)
11. Butchers (Bill Wheeler)
12. Stag & Huntsman Inn (George Gloyne)
13. Kenricks (Viscountess Daventry) (not on map)
14. Manor House (Mrs Stainton)

Appendix 3

Rector Watts reflects on the surrender of Japan : Parish Magazine Sept 1945

News has just come through that Japan has asked for peace. This is the news for which we have been longing and praying for years. It is such wonderful news that I feel almost overwhelmed by it and find it practically impossible to express my feelings on paper. Especially, we all rejoice with those who have relations who are prisoners or internees in Japanese hands. What they have gone through is beyond our comprehension.

But I have one great regret - and I cannot help but say this - it is that we used that most ghastly of all instruments of war - the atomic bomb. The use of it, judging by the correspondence in The Times, has greatly shocked a vast number of people. We all know of course that the atomic bombing may have shortened the war by a few weeks but at what a cost—the indiscriminate massacre of hundreds of thousands of men, women and children. And only a few months, ago we were protesting against the indiscriminate bombing by the Germans in their use of the VI & V2 weapons. Atomic bombing is far more indiscriminate and far more barbarous. Even a number of scientists who helped to produce it have said that often they had hoped that the atomic bomb would not work.

Well, it all goes to show what a ghastly evil modern warfare is. It not only destroys millions of lives and breaks up millions of homes, but it is very apt also to make us lose our own souls. However, one thing we know for certain is that it must be the end of all war or war will end us. So, in our rejoicings let us cast out of our heart once and for all the evil spirit of bitterness, jealousy and fear, and determine to do our best to work for peace and goodwill amongst all men.

Appendix 4

We'll Meet Again : Song by Vera Lynn, music and lyrics by Ross Parker and Hughie Charles.

    We'll meet again

    Don't know where

    Don't know when

    But I know we'll meet again some sunny day

    Keep smiling through

    Just like you always do

    'Till the blue skies drive the dark clouds far away

    So will you please say hello

    To the folks that I know

    Tell them I won't be long

    They'll be happy to know

    That as you saw me go

    I was singing this song

    We'll meet again

    Don't know where

    Don't know when

    But I know we'll meet again some sunny day

Appendix 5

Hambleden Roll of Honour 1939-1945

George Moring
Keith Ansell
Frederick Blackall
Michael Anderson
Roger Hinton
Jack Vaughan
William Purcell
Arthur Wyeth
John Ward

Frank Tilbury
Dennis Belton
Owen Webb
Frank Oxlade
Eric Lovell
Frank Chamberlain
Christopher Beales
John Sumner

RADIO RADIOGRAMS

Amplifiers for Hire.   Accumulators Charged.

PIANOS   **MUSIC**
Tunings.   Records.

BELTON'S
THE MELODY SHOP.

27, Duke Street, Henley-on-Thames,

Telephone 281

G. N. BARTLETT,

Baker, Confectioner, and Grocer : :

FRIETH,

Henley-on-Thames.

Phone Lane End 206.

D. H. LATHAM,

RADIO DEALER

Sets and Accessories.
Accumulators Charged
Car for Hire.

FRIETH POST OFFICE,

Henley-on-Thames.

Phone Lane End 211.

P. H. WARNER

IRONMONGER, DECORATOR & PLUMBER

Sanitary Engineer, General & Furnishing Ironmonger

Station Road, Henley-on-Thames.   Phone 59

UMBRELLA HOSPITAL

New Covers from 3/6   Repairs of all kinds done on the premises   New Umbrellas in Stock

W. A. MORRIS

Saddler and Harness Maker

24, DUKE STREET, HENLEY-ON-THAMES.

EVEREST & SHELDRAKE,

Cycle Agents & Specialists,

Radio Receivers and Accessories.

We specialize in Battery Charging and Repairs.
A Trial Solicited.

63, Bell Street, Henley-on-Thames.

Phone 240.

W. F. ILOTT

Practical
Boot and Shoe Repair Service

95 Bell Street, Henley-on-Thames

—o—

Deliveries in Hambleden District.
All eyes are on your Feet.

TRY PITHER'S BREAD—

Delivered daily to all parts of the Town.

A. PITHER,

High-Class Provisions & Groceries.

49, Bell Street Henley-on-Thames.

Phone 85.

MILLINERY.
General and Fancy Drapery.

H. L. BURNELL

FOR

Hosiery, Gloves, Ribbons, Laces, Corsets, Underclothing, Overalls, Jumpers, Maids' Dresses, Caps, Aprons, Collars, &c.

HENLEY HOUSE—

15 and 17, Bell Street, Henley-on-Thames.

Telephone 48   Established over 100 years

MORGANS Ltd.

General Drapers and Clothiers

MARLOW

Specialize in House Furnishing. Linoleums (laid free). Carpets, Bedsteads, Bedding. Dining Room, Bedroom and Kitchen Furniture. Curtain Fabrics, Soft Furnishings and Household Linens of every description etc., etc.

Estimates Free   Distance no obstacle

G. N. BARTLETT

BAKER, CONFECTIONER and GROCER

FRIETH
HENLEY-on-THAMES

PHONE: LANE END 206

Someone You Can Trust

When it comes to Motor Cars and Radio we think we are that "Someone." We are specialists in all repair work and after sales service. We have a staff of skilled engineers for both departments who use high grade equipment and apparatus. We can assure you complete satisfaction.

R. J. E. PLATT
MOTOR AND RADIO ENGINEER

West Street, Marlow

Phone 215

Stag and Huntsman Inn

HAMBLEDEN

Bedrooms fitted with hot and cold running water. :: Log fires.

LUNCHES ——— TEAS ——— DINNERS

—o—

GARAGE
Minor repairs executed. Oils and Motor Spirits stocked

SALOON CAR for hire, with uniformed chauffeur

—o—

TEL.: HAMBLEDEN 27

Proprietor—G. B. Gloyne
Member, Wine and Food Society

Phone: Lane End 211

D. H. LATHAM
RADIO DEALER

Sets and Accessories
Accumulators Charged
Car for Hire

**FRIETH POST OFFICE
HENLEY-ON-THAMES**

R. B. WAUGH
BOULTER END

High-Class Family Butcher

Home Cured Bacon a Speciality

PHONE: LANE END 281   Daily delivery in Frieth

NATIONAL SAVINGS CAMPAIGN
DEPOSIT YOUR SAVINGS
IN THE
HENLEY TRUSTEE SAVINGS BANK

Established 1816. (Amalgamated with the Reading Savings Bank) Phone 337.

No finer facilities securable.

+ Deposits received up to £500 per annum. + 2½% Interest allowed.
+ Easy Withdrawal Facilities + Government Controlled Services.

25, HART STREET, HENLEY-ON-THAMES.

E. T. SHEPPARD,
(A. A. JONES)

Memorials of every Description in Granite, Marble and Stone erected in any part of the Country.

Any Distance.   *Estimates Free.*   *Established 1906.*

Rockery,   Crazy Paving,   Garden Ornaments.

THE HENLEY MASONRY WORKS,

36, Reading Road (near G.P.O) Henley-on-Thames.   Phone 460

Phone: Henley 531/2

TOOMERS

G.W.R. STATION, HENLEY-ON-THAMES.

FOR COAL, COKE AND PATENT FUEL.

Always at your Service.